*Dedicated to all those who wish to
have a happy and fulfilling family life following the
example of Jesus, Mary and Joseph.*

Table of Contents

Introduction

Dear Friend of Relevant Radio,

I am happy that you have this book in your hands. It will do your soul a lot of good. I know it has done a lot of good for me.

Included in this book are the marvelous reflections on the mysteries of the Rosary by a man who passionately loved God and consciously lived in the presence of Jesus, Mary and Joseph and his Guardian Angel throughout his life: St. Josemaría Escrivá. His considerations bring out the sacred humanity of Jesus as they draw us into a deeper contemplation of the events and circumstances of the Holy Family, as well as the joys and sufferings – physical and emotional – of Jesus. Little by little, you become friends with Jesus, Mary and Joseph, almost part of their household. St. Josemaría prayed the Rosary daily, and when he could, he prayed all of the Joyful, Sorrowful and Glorious mysteries as he walked the streets of Madrid as a young priest. We are grateful that Scepter Publishers has allowed us to include *Holy Rosary* by St. Josemaría in this very special book.

St. John Paul II "the Great" prayed the Rosary daily and often many times a day. I vividly remember him sitting in his chair in a get together with young people in the Cortile di San Damaso on a warm Easter afternoon, listening attentively to the stories of the students, while his right hand was in his pocket fingering the beads of his rosary. If you ever had the chance to meet him – and I am truly blessed as I met him six times between 1984 and 1992 – his secretary would give you a rosary as a memento of the occasion. He was very "Marian" in his devotions, and even his Papal Coat of Arms had the motto "Totus Tuus" (Totally Yours) signifying his singular reliance on the powerful intercession of Our Lady who has interceded for us at critical moments of history to change things for the better. Then, in the sunset of his life, he penned a letter on the Rosary and gave to the Church the "Luminous Mysteries", which might turn out to be what he is most remembered for by the faithful one thousand years from now. We are very grateful that the Vatican has allowed us to include the Apostolic Letter *Rosarium Virginis Mariae* from October 16, 2002, in this very special book. I hope you will read and study the document.

Finally, we've included reflections on the titles of Our Lady from the *Litany of Loreto* which I originally composed in the fall of 2010 to help me stay the course on a 54 Day Rosary Novena at a time when Relevant Radio needed a few breakthrough financial miracles. I expanded upon those reflections when we prayed a 54 Day Rosary Novena "for the needs of the Church and the nation" during the *Family Rosary Across America* from September 8, 2020, the Birth of the Mary, to October 31, 2020, the Vespers of All Saints Day, and that is what is included here. Take them for what they are worth: one man's attempt to dig a little deeper into the treasures of the Rosary. Since I joined Opus Dei when I was 17, I have prayed the Rosary daily, and on occasions, more than once a day.

And what about the *Family Rosary Across America*? When COVID shut things down in March 2020, I went into lockdown too like everyone else, and that practically meant no travel for me. So being stationed in Green Bay at our Headquarters, I decided we would bring the Mass LIVE every day at noon to our audience and that I might as well lead the Family Rosary each evening from our beautiful Chapel of the Nativity at 7pm Central. We had no idea this would be so popular because it's so simple that even a four-year-old can pray the Rosary ... and they do! But it is popular because it meets many needs: the communal praying of the Rosary gathers families together, gives hope, provides comfort, and connects us to Jesus, Mary and Joseph, the Angels and the Saints, and tens of thousands of families across America every evening. This is what "the communion of the saints" means. I am committed to being with you every evening at 7 PM, and thanks to our high-tech team, so far, it has been possible.

A word of thanks to you, our listeners, supporters, and fellow "prayer warriors" – without you, we would not have a *Family Rosary Across America*.

And a final word of thanks to our marvelous team here at Relevant Radio, who work so selflessly and cheerfully in the background to make this possible: Lucas, Patrick, Marty, Mark, Nick, Chris, Scott, Mike, Josh, Jake, Margaret, Sarah, Karen, Suzanne, Jennifer, Beth, Rich, Brendan, Emily, Tim, Steve, Damien, Dan, Nancy, Diana and Rose.

Our Blessed Mother, pray for us!

Rev. Francis Joseph Hoffman, JCD, "Fr. Rocky"
Chairman and CEO of Relevant Radio, Inc.

Meditations From "Holy Rosary"

by St. Josemaría Escrivá

"Take the Holy Rosary, one of the most deeply rooted of Christian devotions. The Church encourages us to contemplate its mysteries. She wants to engrave upon our heart and our imagination, together with Mary's joy and sorrow and glory, the spellbinding example of Our Lord's life, in His thirty years of obscurity, His three years of preaching, His ignominious Passion and His glorious Resurrection. To follow Christ — that is the secret."

St. Josemaría Escrivá
(Friends of God, no. 299)

MYSTERIES OF ST. JOSEMARÍA

Today, as in other times,
the Rosary must be
a powerful weapon
to enable us to win in our interior struggle,
and to help all souls.
Exalt holy Mary with your tongue:
God asks you for reparation,
and for praise from your lips.
May you always want and know how to spread
peace and happiness throughout the world,
through this beautiful devotion to our Lady
and through your watchful love.

ST. JOSEMARÍA ESCRIVÁ
Rome, October 1968

TO THE READER

To say the Holy Rosary,
considering the mysteries,
repeating the Our Father and Hail Mary,
with the praises to the Blessed Trinity
and the constant invocation of the Mother of God,
is a continuous act of faith, hope and love,
of adoration and reparation.

ST. JOSEMARÍA ESCRIVÁ
Rome, 9 January 1973

These lines are not written for "little women." –They are written for full-grown men, and very... manly men, who at times, no doubt, have raised their hearts to God, crying out to Him with the Psalmist: *Notam fac mihi viam, in qua ambulem; quia ad te levavi animam meam.* –Teach me the way I should go, for to you I lift up my soul (Ps 143:8).

I must tell these men a secret that may very well be the beginning of the way that Christ wants them to follow.

My friend, if you want to be great, become little.

To be little it is necessary to believe as children believe, to love as children love, to give yourself up as children give themselves up... to pray as children pray.

And you have to do all this if you are to achieve what I am going to reveal to you in these lines:

The beginning of the way, at the end of which you will find yourself completely carried away by love for Jesus, is a trusting love for Mary.

–Do you want to love our Lady? –Well, then, get to know her. How? –By praying her Rosary *well.*

But, in the Rosary... we always say the same things! –Always the same? And don't people in love always say the same things to each other?... Might it not be that you find the Rosary monotonous because, instead of pronouncing words like a man, you mumble noises while your mind is very far from God?

–Moreover, listen: before each decade we are told the mystery to be *contemplated.*

–Have you... ever *contemplated* these mysteries?

Become little. Come with me and – this is the essence of what I want to tell you – we shall live the life of Jesus, Mary and Joseph.

Each day we shall do something new for them. We shall hear their family conversation. We shall see the Messiah grow up. We shall admire his thirty years of hidden life... We shall be present at his Passion and Death... We will be amazed at the glory of his Resurrection... In a word: carried away by Love (the only real love is Love), we shall contemplate each and every moment of the life of Christ.

For you, my friend, the reader of this book: I have written the *Holy Rosary* to help you and me become absorbed in prayer when we pray to our Lady.

Don't let the sound of words disturb you as you meditate on these thoughts: don't read them aloud, for then they would lose their intimacy.

But do pronounce the Our Father and the Hail Marys of each decade clearly and without rushing: this will help you always to get more and more out of this way of loving Mary.

And don't forget to pray for me.

THE AUTHOR
Rome, on the Feast of the Purification,
2 February 1952

My experience as a priest tells me that each soul has his own path to follow. Nonetheless, dear reader, I am going to give you some practical advice which will not stifle the work of the Holy Spirit within you, if you follow it prudently.

Pause for a few seconds – three or four – in silent meditation to consider each mystery of the Rosary before you recite the Our Father and the Hail Marys of that decade. I am sure this practice will increase your recollection and the fruits of your prayer.

And don't forget to pray for me.

THE AUTHOR
Rome, on the Feast of the Nativity of Our Lady,
8 September 1971

THE JOYFUL MYSTERIES

THE FIRST JOYFUL MYSTERY
The Annunciation

Don't forget, my friend, that we are children. The Lady of the sweet name, Mary, is withdrawn in prayer.

You, in that house, are whatever you wish to be: a friend, a servant, an onlooker, a neighbour... –For the moment I don't dare to be anything. I hide behind you and, full of awe, I watch what is happening:

The Archangel delivers his message... *Quomodo fiet istud, quoniam virum non cognosco? –*But how can this come about since I am a virgin? (Luke 1:34).

Our Mother's voice reminds me – by contrast – of all the impurities of men.... mine too.

And then how I hate those low, mean things of the earth... What resolutions!

Fiat mihi secundum verbum tuum. –Let it be done to me according to your word (Luke 1:38). At the enchantment of this virginal phrase, the Word became flesh.

The first decade is about to end... I still have time to tell my God, before anyone else does: 'Jesus, I love You.'

THE SECOND JOYFUL MYSTERY
The Visitation

By now, my little friend, you have no doubt learned to manage on your own. –Joyfully keep Joseph and Mary company... and you will hear the traditions of the House of David:

You will hear about Elizabeth and Zachary, you will be moved by Joseph's pure love, and your heart will pound whenever they mention the Child who will be born in Bethlehem...

We walk in haste towards the mountains, to a town of the tribe of Judah (Luke 1:39).

We arrive. –It is the house where John the Baptist is to be born. –Elizabeth gratefully hails the Mother of her Redeemer: Blessed art thou amongst women and blessed is the fruit of thy womb! –Why should I be honoured with a visit from the mother of my Lord? (Luke 1:42-43).

The unborn Baptist quivers... (Luke 1:41) –Mary's humility pours forth in the *Magnificat*... –And you and I, who are proud – who were proud – promise to be humble.

THE THIRD JOYFUL MYSTERY
The Birth of Our Lord

Caesar Augustus has issued a decree for a census to be taken of the whole world. For this purpose, every person must go to the city of his ancestors. –And since Joseph belongs to the house and line of David, he goes with the Virgin Mary from Nazareth to the town of David called Bethlehem, in Judea (Luke 2:15).

And in Bethlehem is born our God: Jesus Christ! –There is no room at the inn: He is born in a stable. –And his Mother wraps him in swaddling clothes and lays him in a manger (Luke 2:7).

Cold. –Poverty... –I am Joseph's little servant. –How good Joseph is! –He treats me like a son. –He even forgives me if I take the Child in my arms and spend hour after hour saying sweet and loving things to him!...

And I kiss him – you kiss him too! – and I rock him in my arms, and I sing to him and call him King, Love, my God, my Only One, my All!... How beautiful is the Child... and how short the decade!

THE FOURTH JOYFUL MYSTERY
The Presentation

When the time has come for the Mother's purification, in accordance with the Law of Moses, the Child must be taken to Jerusalem to be presented to the Lord (Luke 2:22).

And this time it will be you, my friend, who carries the cage with the doves. –Just think: she – Mary Immaculate! – submits to the Law as if she were defiled.

Through this example, foolish child, won't you learn to fulfil the holy Law of God, regardless of any personal sacrifice?

Purification! You and I certainly do need purification! –Atonement, and more than atonement, Love. –Love as a searing iron to cauterize our souls' uncleanness, and as a fire to kindle with divine flames the wretchedness of our hearts.

An upright and devout man has come to the Temple led by the Holy Spirit (it had been revealed to him that he would not die until he had set eyes on the Christ). –He takes the Messiah into his arms and says to him: Now, my Lord, you can let your servant go from this world in peace, just as you promised... because my eyes have seen the Saviour (Luke 2:25-30).

THE FIFTH JOYFUL MYSTERY
The Finding in the Temple

Where is Jesus? –The Child, my Lady!... where is He?

Mary is crying. –In vain you and I have run from group to group, from caravan to caravan: no one has seen him. –Joseph, after useless attempts to keep from crying, cries too... And you... And I.

Being a common little fellow, I cry my eyes out and wail to heaven and earth... to make up for those times when I lost him through my own fault and did not cry.

Jesus: may I never lose you again... Now you and I are united in misfortune and grief, as we were united in sin. And from the depths of our being come sighs of heartfelt sorrow and burning phrases which the pen cannot and should not record.

And, once we are consoled by the joy of finding Jesus – three days he was gone! – debating with the teachers of Israel (Luke 2:46), you and I shall be left deeply impressed by the duty to leave our home and family to serve our heavenly Father.

THE SORROWFUL MYSTERIES

THE FIRST SORROWFUL MYSTERY
The Agony in the Garden

Pray, that you may not enter into temptation. –And Peter fell asleep. –And the other apostles. –And you, little friend, fell asleep..., and I too was another sleepy-headed Peter.

Jesus, alone and sad, suffers and soaks the earth with his blood.

Kneeling on the hard ground, he perseveres in prayer... He weeps for you... and for me. The weight of the sins of men overwhelms him.

Pater, si vis, transfer calicem istum a me. –Father, if you are willing, remove this cup from me... Yet not my will, *sed tua fiat*, but yours be done (Luke 22:42).

An Angel from heaven comforts him. –Jesus is in agony. –He continues *prolixius*, praying more intensely... –He comes over to us and finds us asleep: Rise, he says again, and pray that you may not enter into temptation (Luke 22:46).

Judas the traitor: a kiss. –Peter's sword gleams in the night. –Jesus speaks: Have you come out as against a robber, with swords and clubs to capture me? (Mark 14:48)

We are cowards: we follow him from afar, but awake and praying. –Prayer... Prayer...

THE SECOND SORROWFUL MYSTERY
The Scourging at the Pillar

Pilate speaks: It is your custom that I release one prisoner to you at the Passover. Whom shall I set free, Barabbas – a thief jailed with others for a murder – or Jesus? (Matt 27:17) The crowd spurred on by their rulers cry: Put this man to death and release Barabbas (Luke 23:18).

Pilate speaks again: What shall I do, then, with Jesus who is called Christ? (Matt 27:22) –*Crucifige eum!* Crucify him! (Mark 15:14)

Pilate, for the third time, says to them: Why, what evil has he done? I have found no crime in him deserving death (Luke 23:22).

The clamour of the mob grows louder: Crucify him, crucify him! (Mark 15:14).

And Pilate, wanting to please the crowd, releases Barabbas to them and orders Jesus to be scourged.

Bound to the pillar. Covered with wounds.

The blows of the lash sound upon his torn flesh, upon his undefiled flesh, which suffers for your sinful flesh. –More blows. More fury. Still more... It is the last extreme of human cruelty.

Finally, exhausted, they untie Jesus. –And the body of Christ yields to pain and falls limp, broken and half dead.

You and I cannot speak. –Words are not needed.

–Look at him, look at him... slowly. After this... can you ever fear penance?

THE THIRD SORROWFUL MYSTERY
The Crowning with Thorns

Our King's eagerness for suffering has been fully satisfied!

–They lead my Lord to the courtyard of the palace, and there call together the whole troop (Mark 15:16). –The brutal soldiers strip his most pure body. –They drape a dirty purple rag about Jesus. –A reed, as a sceptre, in his right hand...

The crown of thorns, driven in by blows, makes him a mock king... *Ave Rex Judeorum!* –Hail, King of the Jews (Mark 15:18). And with their blows they wound his head. And they strike him... and spit on him.

Crowned with thorns and clothed in rags of purple, Jesus is shown to the Jewish crowd: *Ecce Homo!* –Here is the Man! And again the chief

11

priests and their attendants raise the cry, saying: Crucify him, crucify him (John 19:56).

–You and I..., haven't we crowned him anew with thorns, and struck him and spat on him?

Never again, Jesus, never again... And a firm and practical resolution marks the end of these ten Hail Marys.

THE FOURTH SORROWFUL MYSTERY
The Carrying of the Cross

Carrying His Cross, Jesus goes towards Calvary – called Golgotha in Hebrew (John 19:17). –And they lay hold of a certain Simon of Cyrene, who is coming in from the country; and they make him take the Cross and carry it behind Jesus (Luke 23:26).

The prophecy of Isaiah (53:12) has been fulfilled: *cum sceleratis reputatus est,* he was counted among the wicked: for two others, who were robbers, were led out with him to be put to death (Luke 23:32).

If anyone would follow me... Little friend: we are sad, living the Passion of our Lord Jesus. –See how lovingly he embraces the Cross. –Learn from him. –Jesus carries the Cross for you: you... carry it for Jesus.

But don't drag the Cross... Carry it squarely on your shoulder, because your Cross, if you carry it like that, will not be just any Cross: it will be... the Holy Cross. Don't carry your Cross with resignation: resignation is not a generous word. Love the Cross. When you really love it, your Cross will be... a Cross, without a Cross.

And surely you will find Mary on the way, just as Jesus did.

THE FIFTH SORROWFUL MYSTERY
The Crucifixion

For Jesus of Nazareth, King of the Jews, the throne of triumph is ready. You and I do not see him writhe on being nailed: suffering all that can be suffered, he spreads his arms in the gesture of an eternal Priest...

The soldiers take his holy garments and divide them into four parts. –In order not to tear the tunic, they cast lots to decide whose it shall be.

–And so, once more, the words of Scripture are fulfilled: They have parted my garments among them, and for my clothes they cast lots (John 19:23-24).

Now he is on high... And close to her Son, at the foot of the Cross, stand Mary... and Mary, the wife of Cleophas, and Mary Magdalen. And John, the disciple Jesus loved. *Ecce mater tua!* –Behold your mother!: He gives us his Mother to be our Mother.

Earlier they had offered him wine mingled with gall, and when he had tasted it, he would not drink it (Matt 27:34).

Now he thirsts... for love, for souls.

Consummatum est. –It is accomplished (John 19:30).

Foolish child, look: all this... he has suffered it all for you... and for me. –Can you keep from crying?

THE GLORIOUS MYSTERIES

THE FIRST GLORIOUS MYSTERY
The Resurrection of Our Lord

When the Sabbath was over, Mary Magdalen and Mary, the mother of James, and Salome bought spices with which to go and anoint the dead body of Jesus. –Very early on the following day, just as the sun is rising, they come to the tomb (Mark 16:12). And on entering it they are dismayed, for they cannot find the body of our Lord. –A youth, clothed in white, says to them: Do not be afraid. I know you seek Jesus of Nazareth: *non est hic, surrexit enim sicut dixit,* he is not here, for he has risen, as he said (Matt 28:5).

He has risen! –Jesus has risen. He is not in the tomb. –Life has overcome death.

He appeared to his most holy Mother. –He appeared to Mary of Magdala, who is carried away by love. –And to Peter and the rest of the Apostles. –And to you and me, who are his disciples and more in love than Mary Magdalen: the things we say to him!

May we never die through sin; may our spiritual resurrection be eternal. –And before this decade is over, you have kissed the wounds in his feet..., and I, more daring – because I am more a child – have placed my lips upon his open side.

THE SECOND GLORIOUS MYSTERY
The Ascension of Our Lord

Now the Master is teaching his disciples: he has opened their minds to understand the Scriptures, and he appoints them witnesses of his life and his miracles, of his Passion and Death, and of the glory of his Resurrection (Luke 24:45 and 48).

Then, he brings them out as far as the outskirts of Bethany, and blesses them. –And, as he does so, he withdraws from them and is carried up to heaven (Luke 24:51) until a cloud takes him out of their sight (Acts 1:9).

Jesus has gone to the Father. –Two Angels in white approach us and say: Men of Galilee, why do you stand looking up to heaven? (Acts 1:11).

Peter and the others go back to Jerusalem – *cum gaudio magno* – with great joy (Luke 24:52). –It is fitting that the Sacred Humanity of Christ should receive the homage, the praise and adoration of all the hierarchies of the Angels and of all the legions of the Blessed in Heaven.

But, you and I feel like orphans: we are sad, and we go to Mary for consolation.

The Third Glorious Mystery
The Descent of the Holy Spirit

Our Lord had said: I shall ask the Father, and he will give you another Advocate, another Consoler, to be with you forever (John 14:16). The disciples were gathered together in one room when suddenly they heard what sounded like a powerful wind from heaven, the noise of which filled the entire house where they were assembled. –At the same time something appeared that seemed like tongues of fire; these separated and came to rest on the head of each of them (Acts 2:13).

The Apostles were so filled with the Holy Spirit, that they seemed to be drunk (Acts 2:13).

Then Peter stood up with the eleven and addressed the people in a loud voice. –We, people from a hundred nations, hear him. –Each of us hears him in his own language. –You and I in ours. –He speaks to us of Christ Jesus and of the Holy Spirit and of the Father.

He is not stoned nor thrown in prison: of those who have heard him, three thousand are converted and baptized.

You and I, after helping the Apostles administer baptism, bless God the Father, for his Son Jesus, and we too feel drunk with the Holy Spirit.

The Fourth Glorious Mystery
The Assumption

Assumpta est Maria in coelum: gaudent angeli! –God has taken Mary – body and soul – to heaven: and the Angels rejoice!

So sings the Church. –And so, with that same cry of joy, we begin our contemplation in this decade of the Holy Rosary:

The Mother of God has fallen asleep. –Around her bed are the twelve Apostles. –Matthias in the place of Judas.

And we, through a grace respected by all, are also at her side.

But Jesus wants to have his Mother, body and soul, in heaven. –And the heavenly court, arrayed in all its splendour, greets our Lady. –You and I – children after all – take the train of Mary's magnificent blue cloak, and so we can watch the marvellous scene.

The most Blessed Trinity receives and showers honours on the

Daughter, Mother, and Spouse of God... –And so great is our Lady's majesty that the Angels exclaim: Who is she?

THE FIFTH GLORIOUS MYSTERY
The Crowning of the Blessed Virgin

You are all fair and without blemish. –You are a garden enclosed, my sister, my Bride, an enclosed garden, a sealed fountain. –*Veni: coronaberis.* –Come: you shall be crowned (Song of Songs 4:7, 12 and 8).

If you and I had been able, we too would have made her Queen and Lady of all creation.

A great sign appeared in heaven: a woman with a crown of twelve stars upon her head. –Adorned with the sun. –The moon at her feet (Rev 12:1). Mary, Virgin without stain, has made up for the fall of Eve: and she has crushed the head of hell's serpent with her immaculate heel. Daughter of God, Mother of God, Spouse of God.

The Father, the Son, and the Holy Spirit crown her as the rightful Empress of the Universe.

And the Angels pay her homage as her subjects... and the patriarchs and prophets and Apostles... and the martyrs and confessors and virgins and all the saints... and all sinners and you and I.

THE LITANY

Now the chorus of praise bursts forth in all its splendour of new light and variety of colour and meaning.

We call upon the Lord, upon Christ; we petition each of the divine Persons, and the most Holy Trinity; we speak words of ardent love to Mary: Mother of Christ, Mother most pure, Mother of good counsel, Mother of our Creator, Mother of our Saviour... Virgin most prudent... Seat of Wisdom, Mystical Rose, Tower of David, Ark of the Covenant, Morning Star... Refuge of sinners, Comforter of the afflicted, Help of Christians...

And the recognition of her reign – Regina!: Queen! – and of her mediation: *Sub tuum praesidium confugimus:* we fly to your protection,

O holy Mother of God..., deliver us from all dangers, O ever glorious and blessed Virgin.

Pray for us, Queen of the most Holy Rosary, that we may be made worthy of the promises of our Lord Jesus Christ.

My friend: I have told you just part of my secret. It is up to you, with God's help, to discover the rest. Take courage. Be faithful.

Become little. Our Lord hides himself from the proud and reveals the treasures of his grace to the humble.

Don't worry if, when thinking on your own, daring and childish words and affections arise in your heart. This is what Jesus wants and Mary is encouraging. If you say the Rosary in this way, you will learn to pray well.

APPENDIX

THE MYSTERIES OF LIGHT
Introductory Note

In his Apostolic Letter *Rosarium Virginis Mariae*, the Holy Father John Paul II has indicated that, in order to highlight the Christological content of this Marian devotion, five new mysteries, the "mysteries of light", should be added to the fifteen traditional mysteries.

Holy Rosary, written in 1931, naturally contains no reference to these new mysteries. But throughout his life St. Josemaría lovingly contemplated and preached on these scenes, just as he did with every chapter of the Gospels. Therefore we have included here some excerpts from the writings of the Founder of Opus Dei that make reference to the Luminous mysteries, to help readers meditate on the complete Rosary.

We can show our fidelity to the spirit of the author of Holy Rosary when we pray the Joyful, Luminous, Sorrowful and Glorious mysteries by uniting ourselves to the intentions of the successor of Peter, the Bishop of Rome. *Omnes cum Petro ad Iesum per Mariam!*

† JAVIER ECHEVARRÍA
Prelate of Opus Dei
Rome, 14 February 2003

THE MYSTERIES OF LIGHT

THE FIRST MYSTERY OF LIGHT
The Baptism of Our Lord

Then Jesus came from Galilee to the Jordan to John, to be baptized by him…and lo, a voice from heaven, saying, "This is my beloved Son, with whom I am well pleased" (Matt 3:13,17).

In Baptism, God our Father has taken possession of our lives. He has made us sharers in Christ's life and sent us the Holy Spirit.

The strength and the power of God light up the face of the earth.

We will set the world ablaze, with the flames of the fire that you came to enkindle on earth! And the light of your truth, our Jesus, will enlighten men's minds in an endless day.

I can hear you crying out, my King, in your strong and ardent voice: *ignem veni mittere in terram, et quid volo nisi ut accendatur?* I have come to bring fire to the earth, and would that it were already enkindled! –And I answer, with my entire being, with all my senses and faculties: *ecce ego: quia vocasti me!* Here I am, because you have called me!

God has placed an indelible mark on your soul through Baptism: you are a child of God.

Child, are you not aflame with the desire to bring all men to love Him?

Sources: Christ is passing by, 128; Intimate notes, 1741; The Forge, 264, 300.

THE SECOND MYSTERY OF LIGHT
The Wedding Feast at Cana

Our Lady was a guest at one of those noisy country weddings attended by people from many different villages. Mary was the only one who noticed the wine was running out. Don't these scenes from Christ's life seem familiar to us? The greatness of God lives at the level of ordinary things. It is natural for a woman, a homemaker, to notice an oversight, to look after the little things that make life pleasant. And that is how Mary acted.

Do whatever he tells you.

Implete hydrias (John 2:7), fill the jars. And the miracle takes place. Everything is so simple and ordinary. The servants carry out their job. The water is easy to find. And this is the first manifestation of our Lord's divinity. What is commonplace becomes something extraordinary, something supernatural, when we have the good will to heed what God is asking of us.

Lord, I want to abandon all my concerns into your generous hands. Our Mother – your Mother – will by now have said to you, as at Cana: "They have no wine!..."

If our faith is weak, we should turn to Mary. Because of the miracle at the marriage feast at Cana, which Christ performed at his Mother's request, *his disciples learned to believe in him* (John 2:11). Our Mother is always interceding with her Son so that he may attend to our needs and show himself to us, so that we can cry out, "You are the Son of God."

–Grant me, dear Jesus, the faith I truly desire. My Mother, sweet Lady, Mary most holy, make me really believe!

Sources: *Christ is passing by*, 141; *Letter, 14 September 1951*, 23; *The Forge*, 807; *Friends of God*, 285; *The Forge*, 235.

THE THIRD MYSTERY OF LIGHT
The Proclamation of the Kingdom of God

The kingdom of God is at hand; repent, and believe in the gospel (Mark 1:15).

And all the crowd gathered about him, and he taught them (Mark 2:13).

Jesus sees the boats on the shore and gets into one of them. How naturally Jesus steps into the boat of each and everyone of us!

When you seek to draw close to our Lord, remember that he is always very close to you, that he is in you: *regnum meum intra vos est* (Luke 17:21). The Kingdom of God is within you. You will find him in your heart.

Christ should reign first and foremost in our soul. But in order for him to reign in me, I need his abundant grace. Only in that way can my every heartbeat and breath, my least intense look, my most ordinary word, my most basic feeling be transformed into a hosanna to Christ my King.

Duc in altum. –Put out into deep water! –Throw aside the pessimism that makes a coward of you. *Et laxate retia vestra in capturam.* And pay out your nets for a catch!

We have to place our trust in our Lord's words: get into the boat, take the oars, hoist the sails and launch out into this sea of the world which Christ gives us as an inheritance.

Et regni ejus non erit finis. –His kingdom will have no end.

–Doesn't it fill you with joy to work for such a kingdom?

Sources: Notes from preaching, 19 March 1960; 1 January 1973; Christ is passing by, 181; The Way, 792; Christ is passing by, 159; The Way, 906.

The Fourth Mystery of Light
The Transfiguration

And he was transfigured before them, and his face shone like the sun, and his garments became white as light (Matt 17:2).

Jesus, we want to see you, to speak to you! We want to contemplate you, immersed in the immensity of your beauty, in a contemplation that will never cease! It must be wonderful to see you, Jesus! It must be wonderful to see you and be wounded by your love!

And a voice from the cloud said, "This is my beloved Son, with whom I am well pleased; listen to him" (Matt 17:5).

Lord, we are ready to heed whatever you want to tell us. Speak to us: we are attentive to your voice. May your words enkindle our will so that we launch out fervently to obey you.

Vultum tuum, Domine, requiram (Ps 26:8). Lord, I long to see your face. I like to close my eyes and think that, when God wills, the moment will come when I will be able to see him, not as *in a mirror dimly, but... face to face* (1 Cor 13:12). Yes, *my heart yearns for God, the living God. When shall I go and behold the face of God?* (Ps 41:3).

Sources: Notes from preaching, 4 June 1937; 25 July 1937; 25 December 1973.

THE FIFTH MYSTERY OF LIGHT
The Institution of the Eucharist

Now before the feast of the Passover, when Jesus knew that his hour had come to depart out of this world to the Father, having loved his own who were in the world, he loved them to the end (John 13:1).

When our Lord instituted the Eucharist during the Last Supper, night had already fallen. The world had fallen into darkness, for the old rites, the old signs of God's infinite mercy to mankind, were going to be brought to fulfilment. The way was opening to a new dawn – the new Passover. The Eucharist was instituted during that night, preparing in advance for the morning of the Resurrection.

Jesus has remained in the Eucharist for love ... for you.

–He has remained, knowing how men would treat him ... and how you would treat him.

–He has remained so that you could eat him, and visit him and tell him your concerns; and so that, by your prayer beside the tabernacle and by receiving him sacramentally, you could fall more in love each day, and help other souls, many souls, to follow the same path.

Good child: see how lovers on earth kiss the flowers, the letters, the mementos of those they love...

Then you, how could you ever forget that you have him always at your side – yes, *Him*? How could you forget ... that you can eat him?

–Lord, may I never again flutter along close to the ground. Illumined by the rays of the divine Sun – Christ – in the Eucharist, may my flight never be interrupted until I find repose in your Heart.

Sources: Christ is passing by, 155. The Forge, 887, 305, 39.

How To Pray
The Rosary

"Our Lady has never refused me a grace through the recitation of the Rosary."

St. Padre Pio

How To Pray The Rosary

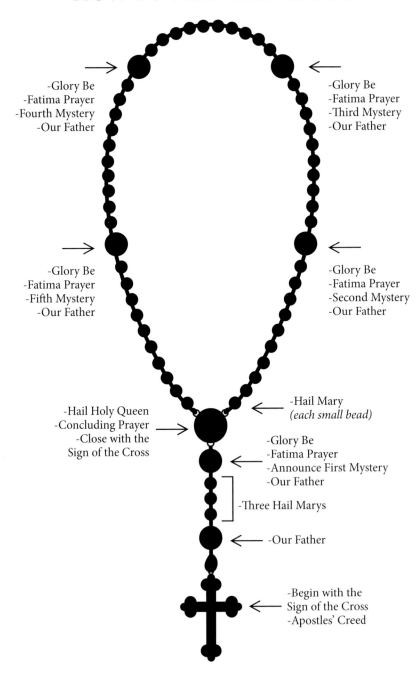

-Glory Be
-Fatima Prayer
-Fourth Mystery
-Our Father

-Glory Be
-Fatima Prayer
-Third Mystery
-Our Father

-Glory Be
-Fatima Prayer
-Fifth Mystery
-Our Father

-Glory Be
-Fatima Prayer
-Second Mystery
-Our Father

-Hail Mary
(each small bead)

-Hail Holy Queen
-Concluding Prayer
-Close with the
Sign of the Cross

-Glory Be
-Fatima Prayer
-Announce First Mystery
-Our Father

-Three Hail Marys

-Our Father

-Begin with the
Sign of the Cross
-Apostles' Creed

Prayers of the Rosary

Apostles' Creed *(begin the Rosary with this prayer)*

I believe in God, the Father almighty, Creator of heaven and earth, and in Jesus Christ, His only Son, our Lord, who was conceived by the Holy Spirit, born of the Virgin Mary, suffered under Pontius Pilate, was crucified, died and was buried; He descended into hell; on the third day He rose again from the dead; He ascended into heaven, and is seated at the right hand of God the Father almighty; from there He will come to judge the living and the dead. I believe in the Holy Spirit, the holy Catholic Church, the communion of saints, the forgiveness of sins, the resurrection of the body, and life everlasting. Amen.

Hail Mary *(say once for each bead in a decade)*

Hail Mary full of Grace, the Lord is with thee. Blessed are thou among women and blessed is the fruit of thy womb, Jesus. Holy Mary Mother of God, pray for us sinners now and at the hour of our death. Amen.

Our Father *(say once before each decade)*

Our Father, who art in heaven, hallowed be Thy Name, Thy kingdom come, Thy will be done, on earth as it is in heaven. Give us this day our daily bread. And forgive us our trespasses, as we forgive those who trespass against us. And lead us not into temptation, but deliver us from evil. Amen.

Glory Be *(say once after each decade)*

Glory be to the Father and to the Son and to the Holy Spirit. As it was in the beginning, is now, and ever shall be, world without end. Amen.

Fatima Prayer *(say once after each decade)*

O my Jesus, forgive us our sins, save us from the fires of hell, lead all souls to Heaven, especially those who have the most need of Your mercy. Amen.

Hail Holy Queen

Hail, Holy Queen, Mother of Mercy, our life, our sweetness and our hope! To thee do we cry, poor banished children of Eve. To thee do we send up our sighs, mourning and weeping in this valley of tears! Turn, then, O most gracious Advocate, thine eyes of mercy toward us, and after this, our exile, show unto us the blessed fruit of thy womb, Jesus. O clement, O loving, O sweet Virgin Mary.

Leader: Pray for us, O holy Mother of God.
Response: That we may be made worthy of the promises of Christ.

Prayer After the Rosary

O God, whose only-begotten Son, by His life, death and resurrection, has purchased for us the rewards of eternal life, grant, we beseech Thee, that meditating on these mysteries of the most holy Rosary of the Blessed Virgin Mary, we may imitate what they contain, and obtain what they promise, through the same Christ our Lord. Amen.

Mysteries of the Rosary

The Five Joyful Mysteries
(Mondays and Saturdays)

           1st: The Annunciation.
           2nd: The Visitation.
           3rd: The Birth of Our Lord.
           4th: The Presentation.
           5th: The Finding in the Temple.

The Five Sorrowful Mysteries
(Tuesdays and Fridays)

           1st: The Agony in the Garden.
           2nd: The Scourging at the Pillar.
           3rd: The Crowning with Thorns.
           4th: The Carrying of the Cross.
           5th: The Crucifixion.

The Five Glorious Mysteries
(Wednesdays and Sundays)

           1st: The Resurrection of Our Lord.
           2nd: The Ascension of Our Lord.
           3rd: The Descent of the Holy Spirit.
           4th: The Assumption.
           5th: The Crowning of the Blessed Virgin.

The Five Mysteries of Light
(Thursdays)

           1st: The Baptism of Our Lord.
           2nd: The Wedding Feast at Cana.
           3rd: The Proclamation of the Kingdom of God.
           4th: The Transfiguration.
           5th: The Institution of the Eucharist.

Litany of the Blessed Virgin Mary
(Litany of Loreto)

"The Rosary is the best therapy for these distraught, unhappy, fearful, and frustrated souls, precisely because it involves the simultaneous use of three powers: the physical, the vocal, and the spiritual…"

Venerable Fulton J. Sheen

LITANY OF THE BLESSED VIRGIN MARY
(Litany of Loreto)

Lord, have mercy. **Lord, have mercy.**
Christ, have mercy. **Christ, have mercy.**
Lord, have mercy. **Lord, have mercy.**
Christ, hear us. **Christ, hear us.**
Christ, graciously hear us. **Christ, graciously hear us.**
God, the Father of heaven, **Have mercy on us.**
God the Son, Redeemer of the world, **Have mercy on us.**
God the Holy Spirit, **Have mercy on us.**
Holy Trinity, one God, **Have mercy on us.**

Holy Mary, **pray for us.**
Holy Mother of God,...
Holy Virgin of virgins,...
Mother of Christ,...
Mother of the Church,...
Mother of mercy,...
Mother of Divine Grace,...
Mother of hope,...
Mother most pure,...
Mother most chaste,...
Mother inviolate,...
Mother undefiled,...
Mother most amiable,...
Mother most admirable,...
Mother of good counsel,...
Mother of our Creator,...
Mother of our Savior,...
Virgin most prudent,...
Virgin most venerable,...
Virgin most renowned,...
Virgin most powerful,...
Virgin most merciful,...
Virgin most faithful,...
Mirror of justice,...
Seat of wisdom,...

Cause of our joy,…
Spiritual vessel,…
Vessel of honor,…
Singular vessel of devotion,…
Mystical rose,…
Tower of David,…
Tower of ivory,…
House of gold,…
Ark of the covenant,…
Gate of heaven,…
Morning star,…
Health of the sick,…
Refuge of sinners,…
Solace of migrants,…
Comforter of the afflicted,…
Help of Christians,…
Queen of angels,…
Queen of patriarchs,…
Queen of prophets,…
Queen of apostles,…
Queen of martyrs,…
Queen of confessors,…
Queen of virgins,…
Queen of all saints,…
Queen conceived without original sin,…
Queen assumed into heaven,…
Queen of the most holy rosary,…
Queen of the family,…
Queen of Relevant Radio,…
Queen of peace,…

V. Lamb of God, Who takes away the sins of the world,
R. Spare us, O Lord!

V. Lamb of God, Who takes away the sins of the world,
R. Graciously hear us, O Lord!

V. Lamb of God, Who takes away the sins of the world,
R. Have mercy on us.

V. Pray for us, O holy Mother of God.
R. That we may be made worthy of the promises of Christ.

Let us pray. O God, whose Only-Begotten Son, by His life, death and resurrection, has purchased for us the rewards of everlasting life; grant, we beseech you, that, we, who meditate on these mysteries of the most holy Rosary of the Blessed Virgin Mary, may imitate what they contain, and obtain what they promise through the same Christ our Lord.
R. Amen.

During Advent
Let us pray. O God, you willed that, at the message of an angel, your Word should take flesh in the womb of the Blessed Virgin Mary; grant to your suppliant people, that we, who believe her to be truly the Mother of God, may be helped by her intercession with you. Through the same Christ our Lord.
R. Amen.

From Christmas to the Purification
Let us pray. O God, by the fruitful virginity of Blessed Mary, you bestowed upon the human race the rewards of eternal salvation; grant, we beg you, that we may feel the power of her intercession, through whom we have been made worthy to receive the Author of life, our Lord Jesus Christ your Son. Who lives and reigns with you forever and ever.
R. Amen.

During Paschaltime
Let us pray. O God, who by the Resurrection of your Son, our Lord Jesus Christ, granted joy to the whole world; grant, we beg you, that through the intercession of the Virgin Mary, his Mother, we may attain the joys of eternal life. Through the same Christ our Lord.
R. Amen.

54 Day Rosary
Novena
by Rev. Francis J. Hoffman, JCD, "Fr. Rocky"

"When you say your Rosary, the angels rejoice, the Blessed Trinity delights in it, my Son finds joy in it too, and I myself am happier than you can possibly guess. After the Holy Sacrifice of the Mass, there is nothing in the Church that I love as much as the Rosary."

OUR LADY TO BLESSED ALAN DE LA ROCHE

Introduction

A little background on these reflections on the *Litany of Loreto*. Back in 2010 we were looking for a financial breakthrough for Relevant Radio, and the path forward was to purchase a major AM station in Chicago, instead of paying rent. On the morning of May 4, I woke up with a very clear idea in my head: "you have to pray a 'super-duper' version of the 54 Day Rosary Novena if you want to get your miracle." Where that idea came from, I have no idea, and I shook my head in quiet disbelief, "you don't pray 54 Day Rosary Novenas, and you'll never be able to do a 'super-duper' version praying all twenty mysteries of the Rosary each day on your own: five Joyful, five Glorious, five Sorrowful, and five Luminous." So, I decided that the only way I would persevere would be to invite others to join me, and I would send them a short email every day with a reflection on the Mysteries, and some commentary on various Shrines of Our Lady throughout the world. That 54 Day Rosary Novena ended on June 26, the Feast of St. Josemaría, and we were on our way . . . halfway there. Later that year I decided to do another "super-duper" version of the 54 Day Rosary Novena commencing on October 16, the Anniversary of the Election of St. John Paul II. To get through this second 'marathon' I invited friends to join me to keep me going, and I committed to sending them daily short reflections on the titles of Our Lady from the *Litany of Loreto*. That is what is included here, but in expanded form explained in the Introduction of the book.

Rev. Francis Joseph Hoffman, JCD, "Fr. Rocky"
Chairman and CEO of Relevant Radio, Inc.

Day 1

Holy Mary, Pray for us!

The very first title in the Litany of Our Lady is the shortest and perhaps the deepest. It's just two words, "Holy Mary", to which the faithful respond, "Pray for us." "Holy" is an adjective to describe Our Lady as dedicated to God. A person cannot be Holy if they are not a friend of God, and of all the friends God has, Mary is His best friend, but she is also our mother. In Latin, the phrase "Holy Mary" is "Sancta Maria" – or "Saint Mary," which is the name of many Catholic churches, colleges, universities, hospitals, and parishes in the world, as well as rivers, roads and mountains. In Spanish, the phrase is "Santa Maria," which was the name of the boat that Christopher Columbus sailed on. We call Mary "Holy" because Mary is full of grace, and grace makes us like Jesus: Holy, Holy, Holy. There's nothing better in the world than to be in the state of grace.

Holy Mary, pray for our Church and the nation.

DAY 2

Holy Mother of God, Pray for us!

Mary is Mother of God because she is the mother of Jesus, and Jesus is God. True God and True Man. The title "Mother of God" is found in the second part of the Hail Mary prayer. It comes from the Greek word "Theotokos" which literally means "the one who bears God" and has been in use by Christians since the 200s in the Holy Land. In the year 431 AD, at the Third Ecumenical Council of all of the Bishops of the Church, held in the ancient city of Ephesus, the Church Fathers proclaimed the first dogma of Our Lady, that Mary is "Mother of God." There was great, great rejoicing when the Bishops, following the lead of St. Cyril of Alexandria, proclaimed Mary the Mother of God. But some Bishops resisted and joined the Nestorian heresy. Within two centuries, their lands and churches would be overwhelmed by the new Islam Religion. If you want to remain strong and steadfast in the faith, repeat many times a day, "Holy Mary, Mother of God, pray for us! Pray for our Church and the Nation."

Holy Mother of God, pray for our Church and the nation.

DAY 3

Holy Virgin of Virgins, Pray for Us!

This is the third title of Our Lady in the *Litany of Loreto*, as we pray for 54 days for the "needs of our Church and the Nation." In our contemporary Western post-Christian culture, virginity is rarely appreciated, hardly expected, and commonly misunderstood as a weakness of character, when in fact, it is the opposite.

Consider the lives and example of some of the great saints who were virgins and completely committed to Jesus Christ: Our Lady, St. John the Apostle, Saint Maria Goretti, Saint Damien of Molokai, Saint Jose Sanchez del Rio, and many others. They all stood strong at the foot of the cross. They all gave themselves without reserve to God at a young age. St. Josemaría had a special insight into the power of the prayer of virgins when he wrote: "Next to the prayer of priests and of dedicated virgins, the prayer most pleasing to God is the prayer of children and that of the sick."

Holy Virgin of Virgins, pray for our Church and the nation.

Day 4

Mother of Christ, Pray for Us!

The first three titles of Our Lady in the Litany begin with the word "Holy," and now the second section has fourteen titles of our Lady that start with "Mother." Three of these titles are relatively new to the Litany, two of them just added more recently by Pope Francis.

The Litany of Our Lady is also known as the *Litany of Loreto*, a small town on the Adriatic Coast in Italy where a major shrine to Our Blessed Mother is located, containing the house of our Lady from Nazareth, where the Annunciation took place. By angelic intervention, that holy house was moved to Loreto in the 13th century to protect it from the violence of the Crusades. This Litany of Our Lady has been prayed there since at least 1531. Today's title, "Mother of Christ," tells us just how important Mary is in the whole history of salvation.

Mother of Christ, pray for our Church and the nation.

DAY 5

Mother of the Church, Pray for Us!

Did you know that it was during the Second Vatican Council that Mary was proclaimed "Mother of the Church?" That's right. It was 1964. Although, St. Ambrose of Milan was already calling Mary "Mother of the Church" in the 4th century.

The Church is the mystical body of Christ, and since Mary is the Mother of Christ, Mary is also Mother of the Church, and from heaven will exercise care and vigilance over the members of the Church, especially when they ask for her powerful intercession. This title, "Mother of The Church" was added to the Litany only recently, in 1981, seven months after a would-be assassin tried to kill St. John Paul II in St. Peter's Square. A marble plaque embedded in the cobblestone plaza marks that spot today, and a window from the Apostolic Palace was bricked up so a mosaic of Our Lady, Mother of the Church, could watch over all of the faithful in St. Peter's Plaza, and memorialize St. John Paul's gratitude that Our Lady saved his life.

Mother of the Church, pray for our Church and the nation.

DAY 6

Mother of Mercy, Pray for Us!

This is one of the newest titles of Our Lady in the Litany, and was just added by papal decree on June 20, 2020. But the title "Mother of Mercy" has been around forever, or at least since the early middle ages. In fact, "Mother of Mercy" is the second phrase of the Salve Regina or "Hail Holy Queen." You'll recognize it immediately. Listen: "Hail Holy Queen, Mother of Mercy, our life, our sweetness and our hope."

It seems very fitting to me that Pope Francis added this title right after the one St. John Paul II the Great added – Mother of the Church – because the extraordinary pontificate of that Polish pope was about God's mercy. In fact, he established a big feast day for the entire Church for the Sunday after Easter. It's known as Divine Mercy Sunday and St. John Paul II died in the Vespers of that day. Every day we pray the Chaplet of Divine Mercy on-air.

Mother of Mercy, pray for our Church and the nation.

Mother of Divine Grace, Pray for Us!

Grace is such a Catholic word! They say you can't see grace because it's invisible, but what do "they" know anyway? I say, you can see the effects of grace. You can see it in a smile, you can feel it in a handshake, you can give it with your helping hand, you can hear it in the kind and gentle and peaceful words of people who walk with Jesus, you can be inspired by it through those who courageously and steadfastly give witness to the Truth. St. Pius X, who had a great love for the Blessed Mother once wrote: "To desire grace without recourse to the Virgin Mother is to desire to fly without wings." So, get it whenever you can: sanctifying grace, sacramental grace, actual grace, charismatic grace, and the state of grace God gives you to carry out your special tasks and responsibilities.

Mother of Divine Grace, pray for our Church and the nation.

Day 8

Mother of Hope, Pray for Us!

This is the second brand new title of Our Lady in the Litany, and was just added by papal decree on June 20 of 2020. Like the new title "Mother of Mercy" this new title is also ancient, and found in the first words of the Hail Holy Queen when we refer to Our Lady as "Our Life, Our Sweetness, and Our Hope." How do you react when you see a little statue of Our Lady in front of someone's house? Or a statue of Our Lady of the Highways near an expressway? Or an image of Our Lady of Guadalupe on a billboard? I rejoice. Every image of the Blessed Mother brings hope because it tells us that Jesus is near. And what does a quarterback do when his team is losing? He fades back, sends the receivers long, and then throws a "Hail Mary" pass and puts his hope in God.

Mother of Hope, pray for our Church and the nation.

DAY 9

Mother Most Pure, Pray for Us!

Outside the entrance to Our Lady of Peace Chapel in Rome where St. Josemaría is buried, you will find a serene white marble sculpture of the Blessed Mother titled "Mother of Fair Love." "She sits as silent sentinel and beckons all who pass by to invoke her maternal intercession for the gift of Holy Purity. A perpetual vigil light nearby signals the power of her intercession for all who wish to be faithful to vows, promises, and commitments of love." That's how I explained it to a visiting Bishop from Texas twenty years ago. He began to weep. I did not understand why. Later we would all know of the broken vows of sacerdotal sons who were never taught the necessity of devotion to their Blessed Mother as an indispensable means to be faithful.

Mother Most Pure, pray for our Church and the nation.

Day 10

Mother Most Chaste, Pray for Us!

It's not that the Church is hung up on sex, or that the Church is prudish. It's simply that the Church promotes and defends human dignity, and recognizes that the human race is the pinnacle of God's visible Creation. Human beings have been created for eternity, to give glory to God.

That's why the Church guards and elevates human sexuality, and protects it in the sacred bond of matrimony. Children have a right to know their mother and father. Children have a right to be born and raised in a family. And the human race is a blessing to planet Earth. That's why the virtue of chastity is necessary. It safeguards sex and places it within the stability of marriage. Sex is always safe, when used as God has intended. Between a man and a woman, open to life, within a marriage. In that context, it is holy.

Mother Most Chaste, pray for our Church and the nation.

DAY 11

Mother Inviolate, Pray for Us!

Inviolate means free from injury or violation. It is not to be confused with the word violet, or the color purple. Just as sunlight passes through a window without breaking the glass, the Blessed Mother remained a virgin before, during, and after the birth of Jesus Christ. That's what inviolate means.

Indeed, the birth of Jesus was a miraculous birth. The Early Fathers of the Church were nearly unanimous in this teaching – St. Ambrose, St. Augustine, St. John Chrysostom, St. Leo the Great, St. Gregory the Great. This title references the second Marian dogma of perpetual virginity. Mary was a virgin before, during, and after Christ's birth. If you believe that I'll tell you another one. That a man can take some bread, say some words, and change it into God. But he can if he's a priest.

Yes, we have some extraordinary beliefs in our Catholic faith. Still, they're all true.

Mother Inviolate, pray for our Church and the nation.

Day 12

Mother Undefiled, Pray for Us!

And we have yet another title in the Litany referring to the miraculous nature of the birth of Christ and the perpetual virginity of Our Lady. While these adjectives sing the praises of Mary, in the background we cannot forget the outstanding protection that St. Joseph offered Her. St. Joseph was chosen by God to protect Mary and the Child Jesus. They lived in very dangerous times, life was short, and people could be brutal. But St. Joseph was always alert, ever obedient, and quick to take action to avoid danger. He was prudent and wise, not just strong. I like to think of St. Joseph as a young man, perhaps twenty years old, a chaste man with excellent self-control, who won the favor of the young maiden because of his virtue and deep faith and goodness. It was this strong and silent faith that allowed St. Joseph to be proven a man of character.

Mother Undefiled and St. Joseph, pray for our Church and the nation.

DAY 13

Mother Most Amiable, Pray for Us!

Mary is the most lovable woman who ever lived on the face of
the earth, and it remains that way in heaven. Our Blessed Mother
is amiable which means "lovable," because she is wonderful.
Magnificent. Awesome. Kind. Friendly. Cheerful. Understanding.
Empathetic. Open. Encouraging. She is never harsh with us, or
bitter, or scolding. Our Blessed Mother always has time for us.
She is very approachable, because she is one of us, and she is
our Mother.

A soul in mortal sin might be ashamed to approach God, but
knows that Mary will smooth things over for him. Even as a
child I recognized the special favor of Our Lady's intercession.
On Halloween, we could always count on getting a full-sized
chocolate Hershey Bar at a neighbor's house on Midway Avenue:
a house with a statue of Our Lady of the Immaculate Conception
in her front yard. Talk about a mother most amiable!

Mother Most Amiable, pray for our Church and the nation.

DAY 14

Mother Most Admirable, Pray for Us!

And what was the most admirable act of Our Lady? Hard to say, really. There were so many … giving an unconditional 'yes' to God's plans at the Annunciation. Visiting her cousin Elizabeth on her own initiative, walking a hundred miles to get there, and then doing chores around her house for three months as if she had nothing better to do. Not uttering a word of complaint on the way to Bethlehem, nine months pregnant and sitting on a donkey, as she reassured St. Joseph, "Don't worry, everything will be fine!" Pushing her way through the crowd to comfort her son as He carried His cross. Standing at the foot of the cross and telling the whole world "He's my son and I love him!"

Admirable. Most admirable. Mater admirabilis.

Mother Most Admirable, pray for our Church and the nation.

Day 15

Mother of Good Counsel, Pray for Us!

This title, added to the Litany by Pope Leo XIII in 1903, refers to an image of Our Lady near Rome which is greatly venerated by the faithful of that region, including Pope Leo XIII and Pope Pius XII, who dedicated his Pontificate that began in 1939 at the beginning of World War II to "Our Lady of Good Counsel."

The well-known image has been venerated since the middle ages and one story tells of its miraculous journey from Albania to a Church in Genazzano, about thirty miles south of Rome. The white scapular is related to this image. And what is the best "counsel" our Blessed Mother ever gave? At Cana, She said, "Do whatever He tells you." Here are five words for us to consider this day. Five words that will change your life.

Mother of Good Counsel, pray for our Church and the nation.

DAY 16

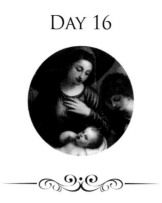

Mother of Our Creator, Pray for Us!

In the twenty-fourth chapter of the Book of Sirach we read: "He who created me has deigned to dwell in my womb." We all know that Mary is the mother of Jesus and that Jesus is God, so Mary is properly called the Mother of God.

But if God is a Trinity, and the Father is the Creator, the Son is the Redeemer, and the Holy Spirit is the Sanctifier, how can we call Mary the Mother of our Creator? Wouldn't that be like calling her Mother of the Father? Not exactly, but you have to know a little bit about the theology of the Trinity to understand this. And that is the Trinity is One, and the actions of One are the actions of All. This is certainly a mystery, but nonetheless true. It's good to have connections in high places. What better connection can you have than with the Mother of our Creator?

Mother of Our Creator, pray for our Church and the nation.

DAY 17

Mother of Our Savior, Pray for Us!

When I think of this title, I imagine Our Blessed Mother standing at the foot of the Cross as Jesus is dying for us and saving the world. And I am grateful for Our Lady's loyal love for her son, and ask her that I may never be afraid to stand up for Him and give witness like her.

St. John Henry Newman, canonized in 2019, explains that Jesus "Our Lord, because He was a Saviour, was a warrior. He could not deliver the captives without a fight, nor without personal suffering."

"Lord, Save Me!" St. Peter cried out in the dark windy night as he began to sink into the terrifying waters of the Sea of Galilee. "Save me, Lord!" we all cry out when we come face to face with our weakness and sinfulness. Only Jesus can save us. And being the obedient Son, He does so immediately when His Mother asks Him to help us.

Mother of Our Savior, pray for our Church and the nation.

DAY 18

Virgin Most Prudent, Pray for Us!

Having reflected on the fourteen titles of Our Lady that begin with the word "Mother," we now turn our attention to the six titles of Our Lady that begin with the word "Virgin." "Virgin Most Prudent" is the first in this section.

Prudence is one of the four cardinal virtues, along with Justice, Temperance, and Fortitude. Prudence is the virtue that resides in our intellect and allows us to choose the right means to good ends. The prudent person listens, reflects, ponders, and then decides a course of action that will give the most glory to God. Important decisions should only be made when you are in the state of grace, and since Mary was "full of grace" we rightly call her Virgin Most Prudent. When you are faced with an important decision, strive to be in the state of Grace, and don't forget to ask Our Lady for advice. "Mary, what do you think?"

Virgin Most Prudent, pray for our Church and the nation.

DAY 19

Virgin Most Venerable, Pray for Us!

The second of the six Virgin titles, "Virgin Most Venerable" is based on Our Lady's declaration of fact – and at the same time a prophesy that has come true. When Our Lady visited her cousin Elizabeth in Ein Karem, St. Elizabeth wondered why she was so lucky to be visited by the Mother of our Savior. Mary then broke out in praise of God and declared in her Magnificat "All generations will call me blessed." (Luke 1:48)

That has come true. Mary is the most famous human being in history. She was famous in the Middle Ages, she is famous today, and she will be famous one thousand years from now. Long after the world has forgotten the names of celebrities, and political figures, and Church leaders who we currently think are important but will soon be in the dustbin of history, Christians will remember and hold in high esteem the name of Mary.

Virgin Most Venerable, pray for our Church and the nation.

Day 20

Virgin Most Renowned, Pray for Us!

There are close to a quarter million Catholic churches in the world today, with an average of 5000 parishioners each. Step into a Catholic church anywhere, and you should always see four things: the Tabernacle, the Altar, the Crucifix, and an Image of the Blessed Mother, usually up in the front, either on the right or the left. Everyone recognizes Our Lady, even non-Catholics. One day some years ago, the then President George W. Bush was cordially greeting supporters and friends at a reception in Washington, D.C. President Bush met a woman from Minnesota who was wearing a small image of Our Lady of Guadalupe on her lapel. With a smile and bright eyes he did a double take and asked her, "Hey, who's that sweet lady on your lapel?" "W" called his wife Laura over and pointed to the image and quipped, "THAT's our girl!!" Most renowned.

Virgin Most Renowned, pray for our Church and the nation.

DAY 21

Virgin Most Powerful, Pray for Us!

We've all heard stories about how a mother can have almost super-human strength when it comes to protecting her young child. Well, Our Lady has more than super-human strength when it comes to protecting us. She has "super natural" strength, so if you need something, pray the Rosary every day for that intention. There's a story that's told about a handsome young man who married a beautiful young woman and then shipped off to war a few days later. Away from his bride in the terrible jungles of the South Pacific, they would pray the Rosary for each other every day. That mutual daily recitation of the Rosary for each other became their lifeline for hope. Four years later he returned, safe and sound, after World War II from the jungles of New Guinea; one of the few men of his company to survive. And he credited all to Our Lady, the Virgin Most Powerful, and the daily recitation of the Rosary.

Virgin Most Powerful, pray for our Church and the nation.

DAY 22

Virgin Most Merciful, Pray for Us!

The title "Virgin Most Merciful" reminds us of Our Lord's words at the Sermon on the Mount: "Blessed are the merciful, for they shall receive mercy." At the end of the world, when we are all lined up for judgment day, and Jesus Christ is sitting on his throne, I don't think any of us will be asking for justice, even if we were part of the "peace and justice" crowd during our lifetime. If we're honest with ourselves, we'll all be begging for mercy. I know I will be. And what is mercy? It means giving people a break, letting them off the hook, giving them a hand, cutting them some slack. Just like Our Lord did with the poor woman caught in adultery. "Woman, has no one condemned you? 'No one, Lord.' Neither do I condemn you." And he never brought up the subject again.

Virgin Most Merciful, pray for our Church and the nation.

DAY 23

Virgin Most Faithful, Pray for Us!

Semper fidelis — always faithful. That is the inspiring motto of the United States Marines who are faithful to country, ready to serve and defend our country to the point of death. The Blessed Mother is always faithful to God, always faithful to Jesus, always ready to stand by Him in the hour of His greatest need. When all of the apostles have fled, except the youngest one, John, Mary is there next to Jesus on the cross, "close to Jesus to the last." At the most humiliating moment in the life of Jesus, when it looked like His entire life had been a complete and utter failure, Our Blessed Mother did not hesitate to stand at His side. A faithful woman makes her husband strong, and a faithful husband will never tolerate the least bit of disrespect for his wife.

Virgin Most Faithful, pray for our Church and the nation.

DAY 24

Mirror of Justice, Pray for Us!

The first of thirteen symbolic titles of Our Lady in the Litany, this calls to mind the magnifying power of a stainless mirror. Christ is the Light, and Mary reflects the light, like a mirror; Christ is the Sun, Mary is the moon; you cannot look at the sun directly, but you can gaze upon the moon. Not far from Mexico City in the ancient city of Tlaxcala, you will find the image of Our Lady of Ocatlan. Behind the main altar of this classical colonial church, is a chamber in the form of an octagon, twenty feet across and twenty feet high, all eight walls covered in mirror. In the center of this chamber, rests a quartz table with a lantern on top. Turn off the lights, light the candle, and the stainless mirrors reflect the light in a brilliant way. But to reflect the light, the mirrors must face the light and be stainless.

Mirror of Justice, pray for our Church and the nation.

DAY 25

Seat of Wisdom, Pray for Us!

I never heard of the Litany of Our Lady of Loreto until I was 12 years old when I attended a summer leadership camp organized by young men of Opus Dei. We would pray the Rosary around the campfire at night and then pray the Litany after the Rosary. As a youngster I thought, "This is interesting, but when is it going to end? These guys never stop praying. Enough already." Now, years later, I hope it never ends. Such a mysterious prayer, so loaded with meaning, running so deep in the rich veins of mystical history. Our Lady, Seat of Wisdom. What on earth is that? "The fear of the Lord is the beginning of Wisdom." And Solomon: the wisest of all. Mary's wisdom is shown in her 'yes' to God at the Annunciation when she comes to visit and help her cousin Elizabeth without anyone asking her to do so. Mary, my mother, teach us wisdom.

Seat of Wisdom, pray for our Church and the nation.

DAY 26

Cause of Our Joy, Pray for Us!

What's the most joyful day of the year? For me, it's always Christmas Day, and the birth of Christ would not have been possible without Our Lady, so that's why we call her Cause of Our Joy. Mary brings Jesus, which means Mary brings joy!

Years ago I toured Frank Lloyd Wright's Falling Waters house in Southwest Pennsylvania. It's a sleek stone home with a waterfall running through it. How cool is that? Still, I felt something was missing in the house as we toured it. It seemed a little cold. Then, walking up the stairs, I noticed a lovely poly-chromed medieval figure of the Blessed Mother and Child tucked away in a niche in the wall. And then I spied a Spanish colonial painting of the Madonna in the Master bedroom. The house was not so cold after all. I sensed the joy that could be found there. Homes with an image of Our Lady are homes of joy and laughter.

Cause of Our Joy, pray for our Church and the nation.

DAY 27

Spiritual Vessel, Pray for Us!

A vessel contains and delivers things. A sailing vessel contains and delivers sailors and cargo. A crystal vessel may contain precious perfume. The more precious the treasure, the more beautiful the vessel. The Blessed Mother contained and delivered the Son of God, and in the spiritual vessel of her soul dwelled the Holy Spirit.

Have you ever wondered why Christopher Columbus named his sailing vessel Santa Maria? He wanted to count on the sure protection of the Blessed Mother on that courageous and daring voyage. If I owned a sailboat, I would call her Estelle de Mati, which means "Morning Star" in Catalan.

Hail Mary, Daughter of God the Father. Hail Mary, Mother of God the Son. Hail Mary, Spouse of God the Holy Spirit. Greater than you, no one but God.

Spiritual Vessel, pray for our Church and the nation.

DAY 28

Vessel of Honor, Pray for Us!

On the mantle in the living room over the fireplace in the home I grew up in, we placed items of honor for all to see: a picture of my grandparents on their wedding day; my brother's diploma from Medical School; an antique clock; a crystal vase; a statue of the Blessed Mother and a statute of the Infant Child of Prague. It is good for us to honor Our Lady, but how? Just as you would honor your own mother.

The same way you would honor your own mother, remember her on her birthday. Bring her flowers. Sing to her or keep a vigil light burning before her image. Write a poem for her … I even know a youngster who brought her a box of chocolates. When he returned the next day and discovered they were still there, he ate them, right in front of the statue of the Blessed Mother. And then, he says, she smiled at him.

Vessel of Honor, pray for our Church and the nation.

DAY 29

Singular Vessel of Devotion, Pray for Us!

What does devotion look like? Some years ago when we started Aquinas Academy in Pittsburgh, I would bring the students to the chapel after lunch to visit the Most Blessed Sacrament. It was wonderful to see how eager and open they were to visit Jesus. Two young girls, in 5th and 6th grade, would always make a beeline for a devotional alcove on the side of the Church which was full of vigil lights and a statue of the Blessed Mother. They would kneel, fold their hands, bow their heads, and pray silently, without a care in the world and no human respect. What a picture of pure devotion.

Both are married now and have children to whom they will no doubt pass along their robust faith. Kneeling, folded hands, and bowed heads: the very picture of devotion! Just like the statue of Mary and her Mother Saint Anne in the Church of St. Anne in Jerusalem.

Singular Vessel of Devotion, pray for our Church and the nation.

DAY 30

Mystical Rose, Pray for Us!

God gives us what we need and He gives us what is good for us. And our Mother – the Blessed Mother – is often pulling the strings.

In a moment of a profound crisis of doubt – doubting if he should flee the terror of the Communists in Madrid during the Spanish Civil War in 1937 – St. Josemaría, for the only time in his life, begged the Blessed Mother to provide some sign he was doing the right thing. He awoke the next morning and discovered a small gilded wooden rose on the floor next to him. And he smiled. The "mystical rose" of the forests and mountains of Rialp. The Song of Songs and the Book of Isaiah tell of a rose blooming in the desert, and in Advent we sing, "Lo, how a rose e'er blooming," all in reference to Our Lady.

Mystical Rose, pray for our Church and the nation.

DAY 31

Tower of David, Pray for Us!

The Tower of David in Old Jerusalem was a mighty tower that defended the City. Tender devotion to Mary, the Mother of God, is the Tower that defends our faith. In the foothills of the Pyrenees Mountains, separating France from Spain, you will find the remains of ancient stone watchtowers, which served as sentinels to warn and protect the Christians from advancing Moorish armies. Charlemagne, Roland, Roncevalles, Covadonga, El Cid are epic names of persons and places caught up in that struggle, the longest war in the history of the world.

The Blessed Mother, of the House of David, is like a strong tower who wards off the attacks of the enemy. Stay close to her by daily devotions – the Rosary, the Angelus, the scapular – and you will keep the enemy at bay, and you will stay strong in the Catholic and Christian faith.

Tower of David, pray for our Church and the nation.

Day 32

Tower of Ivory, Pray for Us!

The Light House of Alexandria was one of the seven wonders of the Ancient World, a mighty tower with a brilliant beacon leading ships safely into harbor. Mary towers over the rest of the human race, and is as pure and flawless as ivory, and leads us to the safe harbor of Christ. The purity of her love and the towering stature of her strength were at their zenith as she stood at the foot of the Cross.

G. K. Chesterton in his poem "Towers of Time" wrote:

> *There is never a crack in the ivory tower*
> *Or a hinge to groan in the house of gold*
> *Or a leaf of the rose in the wind to wither*
> *And she grows young as the world grows old.*
> *A Woman clothed with the sun returning*
> *to clothe the sun when the sun is cold.*

Tower of Ivory, pray for our Church and the nation.

DAY 33

House of Gold, Pray for Us!

I say, "Nothing but the best for God" … like that woman in the New Testament who anointed the body of Jesus. She splurged that day, and broke open the alabaster jar of ointment of pure nard and anointed the body of Jesus. Only Judas complained that it could have been sold for three hundred denarii, about fifteen thousand dollars today, and the money could have been given to the poor. Judas knew the cost of everything but the value of nothing. A golden house for the Lord, a precious tabernacle, an exquisite work of art: that is Mary. But how much would a house of gold cost to build? Just the one thousand square foot floor on the first level at a half inch thick would be $150MM. Imagine that! And Our Lady, the house for the Lord, is a like a house of gold.

House of Gold, pray for our Church and the nation.

DAY 34

Ark of the Covenant, Pray for Us!

Remember the movie Raiders of the Lost Ark and the awesome powers associated with the ark? When the Israelites marched into battle with the ark leading the way, all challengers were vanquished. The ark was made of gold, and contained the stone tablets with the Ten Commandments, a sure path to salvation, and that was known as the Old Covenant. Those who made the effort to abide by that law, were assured salvation. The New Covenant is Jesus, and Mary carries in her womb the New Covenant, Jesus Christ, so she is the Ark of the New Covenant. The Blessed Mother, without stain of sin, is even more precious than gold, and within Her womb She holds the New Covenant, Jesus himself. By the recitation of Her rosary, all who would challenge our Christian commitments will be vanquished.

Ark of the Covenant, pray for our Church and the nation.

DAY 35

Gate of Heaven, Pray for Us!

I had a Jewish professor of medieval history when I was an undergraduate. He claimed to be agnostic, but I'm not so sure. He enjoyed pointing out the "hypocrisy" of the Catholic Church in the Middle Ages, though he did so without malice. Still, I admired the man for his attention to detail, his wit, and dedication: students' essays were routinely returned with more red ink from his pen than the black ink of the typewriter. One day, he lectured on St. Bernard of Clairvaux and Marian piety. "Did you know that the Catholics of the Middle Ages believed that if they wore the scapular of Our Lady of Mount Carmel, that the Blessed Mother would be waiting for them right at the Gate of Heaven, to bring them in, no matter how sinful they were, and she'd say, 'Never mind, this one belongs to me.'" Catholics of the middle ages believed that? Catholics of the 21st century believe that too!

Gate of Heaven, pray for our Church and the nation.

Day 36

Morning Star, Pray for Us!

The morning star, Stella Matutina, heralds the coming of the rising sun, but the morning star is not actually a star, it's the planet Venus, yet it is brighter than any star in the sky. Likewise, the Blessed Mother heralds the coming of Our Savior Jesus Christ, arriving on the scene in history just before Jesus. Just as the morning star, a planet, is brighter than any star in the sky, our Blessed Mother, a human being, shines more brightly in heaven than all of the saints and angels. The morning star is a beautiful thing to behold, and its appearance will make you wonder how God could create something so beautiful. Perhaps in heaven, when we see the Morning Star, we will wonder still. Recently, Pope Emeritus Benedict XVI wrote: "Throughout history, God has never ceased to use Her as the light through which He leads us to Himself."

Morning Star, pray for our Church and the nation.

DAY 37

Health of the Sick, Pray for Us!

Another name for Our Lady, Health of the Sick or "salus infirmorum" in Latin, is Our Lady of Good Health. When we pray the *Family Rosary Across America* on Relevant Radio, the majority of prayer requests are for better health. Some years ago I was at the bedside of a man ravaged by cancer. On his nightstand laid a trusty worn rosary. When the morphine drip could do no more, he would grab his rosary and say, "Oh Mother, help me." And relief, deep and sure, would arrive. The miraculous image of Our Lady of Good Health is next to the tomb of St. Camillus de Lellis in the Church of St. Mary Magdalene in Rome. Many who have prayed fervently before that image could tell you why it is regarded as miraculous.

Health of the Sick, pray for our Church and the nation.

Day 38

Refuge of Sinners, Pray for Us!

Before the days of mini-vans and soccer moms, we kids in the neighborhood would entertain ourselves by playing 'tag', a game that could go on indefinitely, but if you were slow and pudgy it was no fun being "it." Then came the fast guy, and we'd head for the refuge of the monkey bars, also known as 'gool': that was the 'safe zone', a refuge for us little sinners. We all know that Jesus is God, and we all know we are sinners. So, sometimes, when you're a real bad sinner, it's kind of hard to look Him in the eye, and we dodge for cover behind the folds of the mantle of our Mother Mary. She's our Mother; she is our 'safe zone'; she's one of us, because she's human, so she understands. And she takes us by the hand to Jesus. As St. Josemaría wrote years ago, "To Jesus we always go, and to Him we always return, through Mary."

Refuge of Sinners, pray for our Church and the nation.

DAY 39

Solace of Migrants, Pray for Us!

This is the newest title in the Litany of Our Lady, added by Pope Francis: "Friend and Protector of Migrants, Immigrants, and Refugees." There are currently 250MM migrants in the world. They come from all over, and go all over, but the most popular destination is the United States of America. A migrant family faces uncertainty: What does the future hold? Where will we live? What will we eat? Will we be safe? Will we ever return? What all migrants have in common is that they are seeking a better place, a better life, a safe harbor for their family just like Jesus, Mary, and Joseph as they fled Bethlehem and headed to a new a hidden life in Egypt. Mary knew that God would take care of them. And the migrant who turns to Our Lady when in need will be truly blessed.

Solace of Migrants, pray for our Church and the nation.

DAY 40

Comforter of the Afflicted, Pray for Us!

Down through the ages good Christians have suffered, and often they keep such grief to themselves. The unspoken pain of a mother who ponders her son's deep disappointments, the husband who agonizes over his secret infidelities, the son who murmurs silent words of thanksgiving too late at the graveside of his father, and the very real physical pains and discomforts of the poor and downtrodden. But the elderly – often they are the ones who have been most afflicted. Perhaps that is why devotion to the Blessed Mother becomes a welcome relief in old age. The American author Willa Cather put it so well in one of the finest novels ever written, *Death Comes for the Archbishop*. She wrote: "Old people, who have felt blows and toil and known the world's hard hand, need, even more than children do, a woman's tenderness. Only a woman, divine, could know all that a woman could suffer."

Comforter of the Afflicted, pray for our Church and the nation.

DAY 41

Help of Christians, Pray for Us!

St. John Chrysostom called Our Lady "Help of Christians" in the year 345, as did St. John Bosco 1500 years later. Some years ago, as I boarded a flight from Birmingham to Chicago, I sat down next to a young woman who was obviously scared of flying. Noticing my Roman Collar, hope registered on her face. I asked, "You're not scared of flying, are you?" "Yes," she squeaked. Not able to resist my teasing tendencies, I asked again, "Think we're gonna crash and die??" "Yes!!", she cried with fear. So reaching into my pocket I pulled out a navy blue cord rosary; instantly she snatched it from my hand and put it over her shoulders like a necklace and calmed down in a most amazing way! I found out in conversation that she wasn't even Catholic. "Nope, just Christian", she said. And that's what the title means: "Help of Christians."

Help of Christians, pray for our Church and the nation.

DAY 42

Queen of Angels, Pray for Us!

Now begins the final section of the Litany, the 'Queen series', with thirteen titles. The first eight describe saints in heaven and seem to be listed in chronological order: Angels were created first, then patriarchs, prophets, apostles, martyrs, confessors, virgins, and all saints. This title "Queen of Angels" reminds me of a little pueblo founded during the lifetime of a remarkable saintly man: a brilliant scholar, linguist, and missionary, St. Junipero Serra. During his travels up and down the coast of California, he could not ride a horse because of his crippled leg; instead, he just hobbled along. Little did he know that the pueblo where he administered the sacraments, Nuestra Senora la Reina de Los Angeles, would one day be known simply as Los Angeles, the largest archdiocese in the USA. When you pray to the Queen of Angels, remember the Church in Los Angeles.

Queen of Angels, pray for our Church and the nation.

DAY 43

Queen of Patriarchs, Pray for Us!

There were patriarchs in the Old Testament (Abraham, Isaac, and Jacob) and there are patriarchs today, as head of a Church, and as the head of a family. Precisely in an age when the secular culture calls into question the role of the father and the role of the mother – calls into question the complementarity of the sexes, and God's indelible plan for creation – it becomes all the more crucial to foster and honor femininity and masculinity.

What a powerful example the father of a family gives when he leads his family in the recitation of the Rosary. In terms of passing on the practice of the faith, where the father goes, the children follow. If you asked Our Lady, the Queen of Patriarchs, who would be a good model for fathers today, she would say St. Joseph, the greatest of all of the patriarchs.

Queen of Patriarchs, pray for our Church and the nation.

Day 44

Queen of Prophets, Pray for Us!

Do you remember that day when Jesus led Peter, James, and John up a high mountain, and when they reached the top Jesus was suddenly transfigured into a shining and glorious vision flanked by the great prophets Moses and Elijah? Peter was stunned by the majesty and glory of the moment – it was a sneak preview of the Beatific vision – and he didn't know what to say except "Let's build three booths: one for you, and one for Moses and one for Elijah."

He just wanted to freeze that moment for all eternity. And that's what heaven will be like: "Let's stay like this forever." Now imagine Mary, the Queen of the Prophets, reigning over Moses, Ezekiel, David, Isaiah – the four prophets who signaled the virgin birth and are represented at the base of the monument to the Immaculate Conception in Rome. What a vision that will be!

Queen of Prophets, pray for our Church and the nation.

DAY 45

Queen of Apostles, Pray for Us!

I don't think there's ever been a time when it was easy to be an apostle. After all, ten of the first twelve died martyrs. By our baptism, all of us are called to be apostles: to speak the truth and preach the Good News, in season and out of season. We admire the courage and steadfastness of the men and women who persevere in their effort to spread the faith, even when others would undermine their confidence with sneers and mocking comments, and sometimes brutal physical assault.

So where does an apostle find his courage? From the Queen of Apostles, who leads us to Jesus and helps us reflect on His words. Just think about that day of Pentecost and all of the apostles gathered around Mary in the Upper Room. For the modern apostle, a soldier of Christ, his weapon is his Rosary, and his armor is the scapular.

Queen of Apostles, pray for our Church and the nation.

DAY 46

Queen of Martyrs, Pray for Us!

Here are the martyrs that come to my mind: The Missionaries of Charity, the order founded by St. Mother Theresa, in Yemen, March 14, 2016. The 21 Egyptian Coptic Martyrs killed by ISIS on the coast of Libya in 2015. The Coptic Martyrs of Cairo, 2011. The Martyrs of Baghdad, 2010. The Martyrs of Pakistan, 2009. The Cistercian Monks, Martyrs of Tibherine, Algeria, 1996. Blessed Jerzy Popiełuszko, 1984. The Martyrs of Barbastro, 1936. The Martyrs of Vietnam. The Martyrs of China. The Martyrs of Japan. The North American Martyrs, 1646. The Mexican Martyrs. Bl. Miguel Pro. St. Jose Sanchez del Rio. St. Maria Goretti. The Martyrs of Georgia, 1597. The Carmelite Nuns, Martyrs of the French Revolution Reign of Terror. The Martyrs of Rwanda. The Martyrs of East Timor. The Martyrs of Uganda. The Martyrs of the Reign of Diocletian. The Martyrs of Nero. It could be a litany in itself.

Queen of Martyrs, pray for our Church and the nation.

DAY 47

Queen of Confessors, Pray for Us!

And who were the Confessors? They were and are the Christians who gave public witness to Christ even at the cost of difficulty, persecution, torture, and incarceration, but not actually a martyr. Many married people who persevere in their vows are confessors. But a 'confessor' is also a priest who dedicates much of his time to hearing the confessions of the faithful, and when they spend upwards of twenty hours a week hearing confessions in tiny, cramped, uncomfortable confessionals, they too experience a type of incarceration. The Curé of Ars, St. Padre Pio, St. Josemaría, and so many good priests I know 'worked' the confessional. And what did they have in common? Love for Our Lord in the Holy Eucharist, and love for their Queen, the Blessed Mother, the Queen of Confessors.

Queen of Confessors, pray for our Church and the nation.

DAY 48

Queen of Virgins, Pray for Us!

From the Book of Revelation we read, "They are Virgins and these are the ones who follow the Lamb wherever He goes" (Revelation 14:4). In the first Eucharistic prayer at Mass, also known as the Roman Canon, we remember Saints Cecelia, Agatha, Lucy, Anastasia and Agnes. Perhaps one day we will also remember Blessed Anna Kolesarova. They were all virgin martyrs. So was 12-year-old St. Maria Goretti who declared, "No! It's a sin!", to her attacker. She died from the stabbing wounds a few days later, but not before she had forgiven her assailant. She was only 12 years old, but Saint Maria was determined not to give in. I admire her strength. I also admire the strength of Our Lady at the foot of the cross, and St. John at the foot of the cross. Clearly, there is strength in virginity.

Queen of Virgins, pray for our Church and the nation.

Day 49

Queen of All Saints, Pray for Us!

How many saints are there in heaven? I don't know, but I hope a lot. And Mary is Queen of all of them. She is the greatest of all the saints. There's a parish in my neighborhood called Queen of All Saints, and it's famous for its lovely Gothic-style basilica and vibrant parish community. But I must admit it's shocking and amusing to read in the newspaper headlines like, "Queen of All Saints demolishes Our Lady of the Woods." How can that be? Well, usually those headlines are on the sports page and report on the adventures of the basketball or football team from the parishes.

But have you ever noticed how many places and parishes are named after the Blessed Mother? In my hometown alone you will find Santa Maria del Popolo, St. Mary of the Lake Seminary, Marytown, St. Mary's Road, St. Mary of the Annunciation, and in the towns next door, St. Mary of Vernon and St. Mary's in Lake Forest. It's not that Catholics lack imagination. On the contrary.

Queen of All Saints, pray for our Church and the nation.

DAY 50

Queen Conceived Without Original Sin, Pray for Us!

"Conceived without original sin" refers to one of the four Marian Dogmas, known as the Immaculate Conception, defined by Pope Pius IX in 1854, when he said:

> *We declare, pronounce, and define that the doctrine which holds that the most Blessed Virgin Mary, in the first instance of her conception, by a singular grace and privilege granted by Almighty God, in view of the merits of Jesus Christ, the Saviour of the human race, was preserved free from all stain of original sin, is a doctrine revealed by God and therefore to be believed firmly and constantly by all the faithful.*

Our Lady, under the title of the Immaculate Conception is the Patroness of the Church in the United States, as well as the Archdiocese of Chicago. And it was Pope Leo XIII who added this title to the Litany in 1883.

Queen Conceived Without Original Sin, pray for our Church and the nation.

Queen Assumed into Heaven, Pray for Us!

El Greco … Botticelli … Murillo … Poussin … Raphael … All the masters have tried their hand at the Assumption of the Blessed Mother into heaven. For those who love Our Blessed Mother, it thrills the heart and fires the imagination just to envision this event. Each year we celebrate this Solemnity on August 15: a great festival in Italy, and a dearly beloved tradition among the grateful children of Mary at the Shrine of Our Lady of Good Help in Champion, Wisconsin. Oh yes, some skeptics think it's a fraud, that she was never assumed into heaven. "Oh yeah? Then where is she? Prove she's not!" Not exactly a sophisticated theological argument, I grant you that. But it's the one I use. We have claims of relics of the apostles, but no relics of the Blessed Mother have ever been found. This title was added by Pope Pius XII in 1950 with the proclamation of this dogma.

Queen Assumed into Heaven, pray for our Church and the nation.

Day 52

Queen of the Most Holy Rosary, Pray for Us!

So what's the big deal about the Rosary? Isn't it a vain and repetitious prayer? Isn't it rather simplistic? Couldn't just anyone say it? It's rather unoriginal, isn't it? And yet … St. John Paul II prayed it frequently, and he was a brilliant man. Louis Pasteur prayed it, and he too was a brilliant man. The shepherd children at Fatima also prayed it in their own, simple way. It's a simple but profound prayer that unites the family and unites the Church. The Popes have constantly recommended it. Saints have lived by it. And growing up, our family prayed it together each evening. Those were happy days, and so full of life and grace. When folks ask how Relevant Radio is making it, I simply reply: by Our Lady's help through the Rosary. And for the hundreds of thousands who have participated in the evening *Family Rosary Across America* on Relevant Radio, you know how powerful this prayer is.

Queen of the Most Holy Rosary, pray for our Church and the nation.

Queen of the Family, Pray for Us!

St. John Paul II added this title to the Litany in 1995, the Year of the Family, in the hope that Our Lady would protect families from the constant and merciless attacks of an aggressively secular culture. Whenever I visit someone's home I can't help looking for images of the Blessed Mother – a painting, a statue, and icon, whatever. Pleased as punch when I see one, somehow that image of the Blessed Mother tells me there is joy and mercy and hope in that home, even in the midst of occasional sufferings.

All families yearn for unity, happiness and peace, but the absence of grace and the prevailing winds of pride tear apart the bonds of unity. So, what can we do? What can we do? Here's an idea! Gather the family in the evenings and pray the rosary together with us at 7pm Central with the *Family Rosary Across America*. Families praying for families. Families praying with families.

Queen of the Family, pray for our Church and the nation.

DAY 54

Queen of Peace, Pray for Us!

Over one hundred years ago, Pope Benedict XV added this title to the Litany in 1915, during World War I, and it finally came into use in May of 1917, the same month the Blessed Mother appeared for the first time at Fatima. World War I was a terrible, terrible war, a colossal failure of diplomacy and common sense, fueled in equal parts of pride and vanity. Christians killing Christians. Catholics killing Catholics. Miraculously, on Christmas Eve, 1914, there was a brief unofficial truce on the Western front between the Germans and the French, in response to Benedict XV's plea "that the guns may fall silent at least upon the night the angels sang." The soldiers came out of their trenches, laid down their arms, sang "Stille Nacht" in German and "Les anges dans nos campagnes" (Angels we have heard on high) in French, smoked cigarettes, shared brandy, and played ball. For a night – one glorious night – the Queen of Peace reigned.

Queen of Peace, pray for our Church and the nation.

Bonus Reflection

At the time of the first composition of these reflections (2010), there were only 52 titles in the Litany. Since then, Pope Francis has added three more; Mother of Hope, Mother of Mercy, and Solace of Migrants. Since I needed to add two more titles in 2010 to get to fifty-four, I added "Our Lady of the Highways" and "Mother of Perfect Love." Here is the reflection on that last title:

Mother of Perfect Love, Pray for Us!

And who is the Mother of Perfect Love? She is the one who sits next to her children and protects them, guiding them, interceding for them, answering their questions, teaching them, encouraging them, and leading them safely to their destination. She lives only for her children and lays down her life for them. She has no life of her own. Her time is God's time, and God's time is for all who come to her for aid. One day, I might tell you a story about a mother of perfect love I met on a plane.

Mother of Perfect Love, pray for our Church and the nation.

Apostolic Letter
"Rosarium Virginis Mariae"
by St. John Paul II

"The Rosary, though clearly Marian in character, is at heart a Christ-centered prayer. It has all the depth of the gospel message in its entirety. It is an echo of the prayer of Mary, her perennial Magnificat for the work of the redemptive Incarnation which began in her virginal womb."

St. John Paul II

INTRODUCTION

1. The Rosary of the Virgin Mary, which gradually took form in the second millennium under the guidance of the Spirit of God, is a prayer loved by countless Saints and encouraged by the Magisterium. Simple yet profound, it still remains, at the dawn of this third millennium, a prayer of great significance, destined to bring forth a harvest of holiness. It blends easily into the spiritual journey of the Christian life, which, after two thousand years, has lost none of the freshness of its beginnings and feels drawn by the Spirit of God to "set out into the deep" (*duc in altum!*) in order once more to proclaim, and even cry out, before the world that Jesus Christ is Lord and Saviour, "the way, and the truth and the life" (*Jn* 14:6), "the goal of human history and the point on which the desires of history and civilization turn".[1]

The Rosary, though clearly Marian in character, is at heart a Christocentric prayer. In the sobriety of its elements, it has all the *depth of the Gospel message in its entirety*, of which it can be said to be a compendium.[2] It is an echo of the prayer of Mary, her perennial *Magnificat* for the work of the redemptive Incarnation which began in her virginal womb. With the Rosary, the Christian people *sits at the school of Mary* and is led to contemplate the beauty on the face of Christ and to experience the depths of his love. Through the Rosary the faithful receive abundant grace, as though from the very hands of the Mother of the Redeemer.

The Popes and the Rosary

2. Numerous predecessors of mine attributed great importance to this prayer. Worthy of special note in this regard is Pope Leo XIII who on 1 September 1883 promulgated the Encyclical *Supremi Apostolatus Officio*,[3] a document of great worth, the first of his many statements about this prayer, in which he proposed the Rosary as an effective spiritual weapon against the evils afflicting society. Among the more recent Popes who, from the time of the Second Vatican Council, have distinguished themselves in promoting the Rosary, I would mention Blessed John XXIII[4] and above all Pope Paul VI, who in his Apostolic Exhortation *Marialis Cultus* emphasized, in the spirit of the Second Vatican Council, the Rosary's evangelical character and its

Christocentric inspiration. I myself have often encouraged the frequent recitation of the Rosary. From my youthful years this prayer has held an important place in my spiritual life. I was powerfully reminded of this during my recent visit to Poland, and in particular at the Shrine of Kalwaria. The Rosary has accompanied me in moments of joy and in moments of difficulty. To it I have entrusted any number of concerns; in it I have always found comfort. Twenty-four years ago, on 29 October 1978, scarcely two weeks after my election to the See of Peter, I frankly admitted: "The Rosary is my favourite prayer. A marvellous prayer! Marvellous in its simplicity and its depth. [...]. It can be said that the Rosary is, in some sense, a prayer-commentary on the final chapter of the Vatican II Constitution *Lumen Gentium*, a chapter which discusses the wondrous presence of the Mother of God in the mystery of Christ and the Church. Against the background of the words *Ave Maria* the principal events of the life of Jesus Christ pass before the eyes of the soul. They take shape in the complete series of the joyful, sorrowful and glorious mysteries, and they put us in living communion with Jesus through – we might say – the heart of his Mother. At the same time our heart can embrace in the decades of the Rosary all the events that make up the lives of individuals, families, nations, the Church, and all mankind. Our personal concerns and those of our neighbour, especially those who are closest to us, who are dearest to us. Thus the simple prayer of the Rosary marks the rhythm of human life".[5]

With these words, dear brothers and sisters, I set *the first year of my Pontificate* within the daily rhythm of the Rosary. Today, *as I begin the twenty-fifth year of my service as the Successor of Peter*, I wish to do the same. How many graces have I received in these years from the Blessed Virgin through the Rosary: *Magnificat anima mea Dominum!* I wish to lift up my thanks to the Lord in the words of his Most Holy Mother, under whose protection I have placed my Petrine ministry: *Totus Tuus!*

October 2002 – October 2003: The Year of the Rosary

3. Therefore, in continuity with my reflection in the Apostolic Letter *Novo Millennio Ineunte*, in which, after the experience of the Jubilee, I invited the people of God to "start afresh from Christ",[6] I have felt drawn to offer a reflection on the Rosary, as a kind of Marian complement to that Letter and an exhortation to contemplate the face

of Christ in union with, and at the school of, his Most Holy Mother. To recite the Rosary is nothing other than to *contemplate with Mary the face of Christ.* As a way of highlighting this invitation, prompted by the forthcoming 120th anniversary of the aforementioned Encyclical of Leo XIII, I desire that during the course of this year the Rosary should be especially emphasized and promoted in the various Christian communities. I therefore proclaim the year from October 2002 to October 2003 *the Year of the Rosary.*

I leave this pastoral proposal to the initiative of each ecclesial community. It is not my intention to encumber but rather to complete and consolidate pastoral programmes of the Particular Churches. I am confident that the proposal will find a ready and generous reception. The Rosary, reclaimed in its full meaning, goes to the very heart of Christian life; it offers a familiar yet fruitful spiritual and educational opportunity for personal contemplation, the formation of the People of God, and the new evangelization. I am pleased to reaffirm this also in the joyful remembrance of another anniversary: the fortieth anniversary of the opening of the Second Vatican Ecumenical Council on October 11, 1962, the "great grace" disposed by the Spirit of God for the Church in our time.[7]

Objections to the Rosary

4. The timeliness of this proposal is evident from a number of considerations. First, the urgent need to counter a certain crisis of the Rosary, which in the present historical and theological context can risk being wrongly devalued, and therefore no longer taught to the younger generation. There are some who think that the centrality of the Liturgy, rightly stressed by the Second Vatican Ecumenical Council, necessarily entails giving lesser importance to the Rosary. Yet, as Pope Paul VI made clear, not only does this prayer not conflict with the Liturgy, *it sustains it,* since it serves as an excellent introduction and a faithful echo of the Liturgy, enabling people to participate fully and interiorly in it and to reap its fruits in their daily lives.

Perhaps too, there are some who fear that the Rosary is somehow unecumenical because of its distinctly Marian character. Yet the Rosary clearly belongs to the kind of veneration of the Mother of God described by the Council: a devotion directed to the Christological centre of the Christian faith, in such a way that "when the Mother is honoured, the Son ... is duly known, loved and glorified".[8] If properly revitalized, the Rosary is an aid and certainly not a hindrance to ecumenism!

A path of contemplation

5. But the most important reason for strongly encouraging the practice of the Rosary is that it represents a most effective means of fostering among the faithful that *commitment to the contemplation of the Christian mystery* which I have proposed in the Apostolic Letter *Novo Millennio Ineunte* as a genuine "training in holiness": "What is needed is a Christian life distinguished above all in the *art of prayer*".[9] Inasmuch as contemporary culture, even amid so many indications to the contrary, has witnessed the flowering of a new call for spirituality, due also to the influence of other religions, it is more urgent than ever that our Christian communities should become "genuine schools of prayer".[10]

The Rosary belongs among the finest and most praiseworthy traditions of Christian contemplation. Developed in the West, it is a typically meditative prayer, corresponding in some way to the "prayer of the heart" or "Jesus prayer" which took root in the soil of the Christian East.

Prayer for peace and for the family

6. A number of historical circumstances also make a revival of the Rosary quite timely. First of all, the need to implore from *God the gift of peace*. The Rosary has many times been proposed by my predecessors and myself as a prayer for peace. At the start of a millennium which began with the terrifying attacks of 11 September 2001, a millennium which witnesses every day innumerous parts of the world fresh scenes of bloodshed and violence, to rediscover the Rosary means to immerse oneself in contemplation of the mystery of Christ who "is our peace", since he made "the two of us one, and broke down the dividing wall of hostility" (*Eph* 2:14). Consequently, one cannot recite the Rosary without feeling caught up in a clear commitment to advancing peace,

especially in the land of Jesus, still so sorely afflicted and so close to the heart of every Christian.

A similar need for commitment and prayer arises in relation to another critical contemporary issue: *the family*, the primary cell of society, increasingly menaced by forces of disintegration on both the ideological and practical planes, so as to make us fear for the future of this fundamental and indispensable institution and, with it, for the future of society as a whole. The revival of the Rosary in Christian families, within the context of a broader pastoral ministry to the family, will be an effective aid to countering the devastating effects of this crisis typical of our age.

"Behold, your Mother!" (*Jn* 19:27)

7. Many signs indicate that still today the Blessed Virgin desires to exercise through this same prayer that maternal concern to which the dying Redeemer entrusted, in the person of the beloved disciple, all the sons and daughters of the Church: "Woman, behold your son!" (*Jn* 19:26). Well-known are the occasions in the nineteenth and the twentieth centuries on which the Mother of Christ made her presence felt and her voice heard, in order to exhort the People of God to this form of contemplative prayer. I would mention in particular, on account of their great influence on the lives of Christians and the authoritative recognition they have received from the Church, the apparitions of Lourdes and of Fatima;[11] these shrines continue to be visited by great numbers of pilgrims seeking comfort and hope.

Following the witnesses

8. It would be impossible to name all the many Saints who discovered in the Rosary a genuine path to growth in holiness. We need but mention Saint Louis Marie Grignion de Montfort, the author of an excellent work on the Rosary,[12] and, closer to ourselves, Padre Pio of Pietrelcina, whom I recently had the joy of canonizing. As a true apostle of the Rosary, Blessed Bartolo Longo had a special charism. His path to holiness rested on an inspiration heard in the depths of his heart: "Whoever spreads the Rosary is saved!".[13] As a result, he felt called to build a Church dedicated to Our Lady of the Holy Rosary in

Pompei, against the background of the ruins of the ancient city, which scarcely heard the proclamation of Christ before being buried in 79 A.D. during an eruption of Mount Vesuvius, only to emerge centuries later from its ashes as a witness to the lights and shadows of classical civilization. By his whole life's work and especially by the practice of the "Fifteen Saturdays", Bartolo Longo promoted the Christocentric and contemplative heart of the Rosary, and received great encouragement and support from Leo XIII, the "Pope of the Rosary".

CHAPTER I
Contemplating Christ with Mary

A face radiant as the sun

9. "And he was transfigured before them, and his face shone like the sun" (*Mt* 17:2). The Gospel scene of Christ's transfiguration, in which the three Apostles Peter, James and John appear entranced by the beauty of the Redeemer, can be seen as *an icon of Christian contemplation*. To look upon the face of Christ, to recognize its mystery amid the daily events and the sufferings of his human life, and then to grasp the divine splendour definitively revealed in the Risen Lord, seated in glory at the right hand of the Father: this is the task of every follower of Christ and therefore the task of each one of us. In contemplating Christ's face we become open to receiving the mystery of Trinitarian life, experiencing ever anew the love of the Father and delighting in the joy of the Holy Spirit. Saint Paul's words can then be applied to us: "Beholding the glory of the Lord, we are being changed into his likeness, from one degree of glory to another; for this comes from the Lord who is the Spirit" (*2Cor* 3:18).

Mary, model of contemplation

10. The contemplation of Christ has an *incomparable model* in Mary. In a unique way the face of the Son belongs to Mary. It was in her womb that Christ was formed, receiving from her a human resemblance which points to an even greater spiritual closeness. No one has ever devoted himself to the contemplation of the face of Christ as faithfully as Mary. The eyes of her heart already turned to him at the Annunciation, when

she conceived him by the power of the Holy Spirit. In the months that followed she began to sense his presence and to picture his features. When at last she gave birth to him in Bethlehem, her eyes were able to gaze tenderly on the face of her Son, as she "wrapped him in swaddling cloths, and laid him in a manger" (*Lk* 2:7).

Thereafter Mary's gaze, ever filled with adoration and wonder, would never leave him. At times it would be a *questioning look*, as in the episode of the finding in the Temple: "Son, why have you treated us so?" (Lk 2:48); it would always be a *penetrating gaze*, one capable of deeply understanding Jesus, even to the point of perceiving his hidden feelings and anticipating his decisions, as at Cana (cf. *Jn* 2:5). At other times it would be a *look of sorrow*, especially beneath the Cross, where her vision would still be that of a mother giving birth, for Mary not only shared the passion and death of her Son, she also received the new son given to her in the beloved disciple (cf. *Jn* 19:26-27). On the morning of Easter hers would be *a gaze radiant with the joy of the Resurrection*, and finally, on the day of Pentecost, *a gaze afire* with the outpouring of the Spirit (cf. *Acts* 1:14).

Mary's memories

11. Mary lived with her eyes fixed on Christ, treasuring his every word: "She kept all these things, pondering them in her heart" (*Lk* 2:19; cf. 2:51). The memories of Jesus, impressed upon her heart, were always with her, leading her to reflect on the various moments of her life at her Son's side. In a way those memories were to be the "rosary" which she recited uninterruptedly throughout her earthly life.

Even now, amid the joyful songs of the heavenly Jerusalem, the reasons for her thanksgiving and praise remain unchanged. They inspire her maternal concern for the pilgrim Church, in which she continues to relate her personal account of the Gospel. *Mary constantly sets before the faithful the "mysteries" of her Son*, with the desire that the contemplation of those mysteries will release all their saving power. In the recitation of the Rosary, the Christian community enters into contact with the memories and the contemplative gaze of Mary.

The Rosary, a contemplative prayer

12. The Rosary, precisely because it starts with Mary's own experience, is *an exquisitely contemplative prayer*. Without this contemplative dimension, it would lose its meaning, as Pope Paul VI clearly pointed out: "Without contemplation, the Rosary is a body without a soul, and its recitation runs the risk of becoming a mechanical repetition of formulas, in violation of the admonition of Christ: 'In praying do not heap up empty phrases as the Gentiles do; for they think they will be heard for their many words' (*Mt* 6:7). By its nature the recitation of the Rosary calls for a quiet rhythm and a lingering pace, helping the individual to meditate on the mysteries of the Lord's life as seen through the eyes of her who was closest to the Lord. In this way the unfathomable riches of these mysteries are disclosed".[14]

It is worth pausing to consider this profound insight of Paul VI, in order to bring out certain aspects of the Rosary which show that it is really a form of Christocentric contemplation.

Remembering Christ with Mary

13. Mary's contemplation is above all *a remembering*. We need to understand this word in the biblical sense of remembrance (*zakar*) as a making present of the works brought about by God in the history of salvation. The Bible is an account of saving events culminating in Christ himself. These events not only belong to "yesterday"; *they are also part of the "today" of salvation*. This making present comes about above all in the Liturgy: what God accomplished centuries ago did not only affect the direct witnesses of those events; it continues to affect people in every age with its gift of grace. To some extent this is also true of every other devout approach to those events: to "remember" them in a spirit of faith and love is to be open to the grace which Christ won for us by the mysteries of his life, death and resurrection.

Consequently, while it must be reaffirmed with the Second Vatican Council that the Liturgy, as the exercise of the priestly office of Christ and an act of public worship, is "the summit to which the activity of the Church is directed and the font from which all its power flows",[15] it is also necessary to recall that the spiritual life "is not limited solely to participation in the liturgy. Christians, while they are called to prayer in common, must also go to their own rooms to pray to their Father in secret (cf. *Mt* 6:6); indeed, according to the teaching of the Apostle, they must pray without ceasing (cf. *1 Thes* 5:17)".[16] The Rosary, in its own particular way, is part of this varied panorama of "ceaseless" prayer. If the Liturgy, as the activity of Christ and the Church, is *a saving action par excellence*, the Rosary too, as a "meditation" with Mary on Christ, is *a salutary contemplation*. By immersing us in the mysteries of the Redeemer's life, it ensures that what he has done and what the liturgy makes present is profoundly assimilated and shapes our existence.

Learning Christ from Mary

14. Christ is the supreme Teacher, the revealer and the one revealed. It is not just a question of learning what he taught but of *"learning him"*. In this regard could we have any better teacher than Mary? From the divine standpoint, the Spirit is the interior teacher who leads us to the full truth of Christ (cf. *Jn* 14:26; 15:26; 16:13). But among creatures no one knows Christ better than Mary; no one can introduce us to a profound knowledge of his mystery better than his Mother.

The first of the "signs" worked by Jesus – the changing of water into wine at the marriage in Cana – clearly presents Mary in the guise of a teacher, as she urges the servants to do what Jesus commands (cf. *Jn* 2:5). We can imagine that she would have done likewise for the disciples after Jesus' Ascension, when she joined them in awaiting the Holy Spirit and supported them in their first mission. Contemplating the scenes of the Rosary in union with Mary is a means of learning from her to "read" Christ, to discover his secrets and to understand his message.

This school of Mary is all the more effective if we consider that she teaches by obtaining for us in abundance the gifts of the Holy Spirit, even as she offers us the incomparable example of her own "pilgrimage of faith".[17] As we contemplate each mystery of her Son's life, she invites us to do as she did at the Annunciation: to ask humbly the questions which open us to the light, in order to end with the obedience of faith: "Behold I am the handmaid of the Lord; be it done to me according to your word" (*Lk* 1:38).

Being conformed to Christ with Mary

15. Christian spirituality is distinguished by the disciple's commitment to become conformed ever more fully to his Master (cf. *Rom* 8:29; *Phil* 3:10,12). The outpouring of the Holy Spirit in Baptism grafts the believer like a branch onto the vine which is Christ (cf. *Jn* 15:5) and makes him a member of Christ's mystical Body (cf. *1Cor* 12:12; *Rom* 12:5). This initial unity, however, calls for a growing assimilation which will increasingly shape the conduct of the disciple in accordance with the "mind" of Christ: "Have this mind among yourselves, which was in Christ Jesus" (*Phil* 2:5). In the words of the Apostle, we are called "to put on the Lord Jesus Christ" (cf. *Rom* 13:14; *Gal* 3:27).

In the spiritual journey of the Rosary, based on the constant contemplation – in Mary's company – of the face of Christ, this demanding ideal of being conformed to him is pursued through an association which could be described in terms of friendship. We are thereby enabled to enter naturally into Christ's life and as it were to share his deepest feelings. In this regard Blessed Bartolo Longo has written: "Just as two friends, frequently in each other's company, tend to develop similar habits, so too, by holding familiar converse with Jesus and the Blessed Virgin, by meditating on the mysteries of the Rosary and by living the same life in Holy Communion, we can become, to the extent of our lowliness, similar to them and can learn from these supreme models a life of humility, poverty, hiddenness, patience and perfection".[(18)]

In this process of being conformed to Christ in the Rosary, we entrust ourselves in a special way to the maternal care of the Blessed Virgin. She who is both the Mother of Christ and a member of the Church, indeed her "pre-eminent and altogether singular member",[(19)] is at the same time the "Mother of the Church". As such, she continually brings to birth children for the mystical Body of her Son. She does so through her intercession, imploring upon them the inexhaustible outpouring of the Spirit. Mary is *the perfect icon of the motherhood of the Church*.

The Rosary mystically transports us to Mary's side as she is busy watching over the human growth of Christ in the home of Nazareth. This enables her to train us and to mold us with the same care, until

Christ is "fully formed" in us (cf. *Gal* 4:19). This role of Mary, totally grounded in that of Christ and radically subordinated to it, "in no way obscures or diminishes the unique mediation of Christ, but rather shows its power".[20] This is the luminous principle expressed by the Second Vatican Council which I have so powerfully experienced in my own life and have made the basis of my episcopal motto: *Totus Tuus*.[21] The motto is of course inspired by the teaching of Saint Louis Marie Grignion de Montfort, who explained in the following words Mary's role in the process of our configuration to Christ: "*Our entire perfection consists in being conformed, united and consecrated to Jesus Christ*. Hence the most perfect of all devotions is undoubtedly that which conforms, unites and consecrates us most perfectly to Jesus Christ. Now, since Mary is of all creatures the one most conformed to Jesus Christ, it follows that among all devotions that which most consecrates and conforms a soul to our Lord is devotion to Mary, his Holy Mother, and that the more a soul is consecrated to her the more will it be consecrated to Jesus Christ".[22] Never as in the Rosary do the life of Jesus and that of Mary appear so deeply joined. Mary lives only in Christ and for Christ!

Praying to Christ with Mary

16. Jesus invited us to turn to God with insistence and the confidence that we will be heard: "Ask, and it will be given to you; seek, and you will find; knock, and it will be opened to you" (*Mt* 7:7). The basis for this power of prayer is the goodness of the Father, but also the mediation of Christ himself (cf. *1Jn* 2:1) and the working of the Holy Spirit who "intercedes for us" according to the will of God (cf. *Rom* 8:26-27). For "we do not know how to pray as we ought" (Rom 8:26), and at times we are not heard "because we ask wrongly" (cf. *Jas* 4:2-3).

In support of the prayer which Christ and the Spirit cause to rise in our hearts, Mary intervenes with her maternal intercession. "The prayer of the Church is sustained by the prayer of Mary".[23] If Jesus, the one Mediator, is the Way of our prayer, then Mary, his purest and most transparent reflection, shows us the Way. "Beginning with Mary's unique cooperation with the working of the Holy Spirit, the Churches developed their prayer to the Holy Mother of God, centering it on the person of Christ manifested in his mysteries".[24] At the wedding of Cana the Gospel clearly shows the power of Mary's intercession as she makes known to Jesus the needs of others: "They have no wine" (*Jn* 2:3).

The Rosary is both meditation and supplication. Insistent prayer to the Mother of God is based on confidence that her maternal intercession can obtain all things from the heart of her Son. She is "all-powerful by grace", to use the bold expression, which needs to be properly understood, of Blessed Bartolo Longo in his *Supplication to Our Lady*.[25] This is a conviction which, beginning with the Gospel, has grown ever more firm in the experience of the Christian people. The supreme poet Dante expresses it marvellously in the lines sung by Saint Bernard: "Lady, thou art so great and so powerful, that whoever desires grace yet does not turn to thee, would have his desire fly without wings".[26] When in the Rosary we plead with Mary, the sanctuary of the Holy Spirit (cf. *Lk* 1:35), she intercedes for us before the Father who filled her with grace and before the Son born of her womb, praying with us and for us.

Proclaiming Christ with Mary

17. The Rosary is also a *path of proclamation* and increasing knowledge, in which the mystery of Christ is presented again and again at different levels of the Christian experience. Its form is that of a prayerful and contemplative presentation, capable of forming Christians according to the heart of Christ. When the recitation of the Rosary combines all the elements needed for an effective meditation, especially in its communal celebration in parishes and shrines, it can present *a significant catechetical opportunity* which pastors should use to advantage. In this way too Our Lady of the Rosary continues her work of proclaiming Christ. The history of the Rosary shows how this prayer was used in particular by the Dominicans at a difficult time for the Church due to the spread of heresy. Today we are facing new challenges. Why should we not once more have recourse to the Rosary, with the same faith as those who have gone before us? The Rosary retains all its power and continues to be a valuable pastoral resource for every good evangelizer.

CHAPTER II
Mysteries of Christ – Mysteries of His Mother

The Rosary, "a compendium of the Gospel"

18. The only way to approach the contemplation of Christ's face is by listening in the Spirit to the Father's voice, since "no one knows the Son except the Father" (*Mt* 11:27). In the region of Caesarea Philippi, Jesus responded to Peter's confession of faith by indicating the source of that clear intuition of his identity: "Flesh and blood has not revealed this to you, but my Father who is in heaven" (*Mt* 16:17). What is needed, then, is a revelation from above. In order to receive that revelation, attentive listening is indispensable: "Only *the experience of silence and prayer* offers the proper setting for the growth and development of a true, faithful and consistent knowledge of that mystery".[(27)]

The Rosary is one of the traditional paths of Christian prayer directed to the contemplation of Christ's face. Pope Paul VI described it in these words: "As a Gospel prayer, centred on the mystery of the redemptive Incarnation, the Rosary is a prayer with a clearly Christological orientation. Its most characteristic element, in fact, the litany – like succession of *Hail Marys*, becomes in itself an unceasing praise of Christ, who is the ultimate object both of the Angel's announcement and of the greeting of the Mother of John the Baptist: 'Blessed is the fruit of your womb' (*Lk* 1:42). We would go further and say that the succession of *Hail Marys* constitutes the warp on which is woven the contemplation of the mysteries. The Jesus that each *Hail Mary* recalls is the same Jesus whom the succession of mysteries proposes to us now as the Son of God, now as the Son of the Virgin".[(28)]

A proposed addition to the traditional pattern

19. Of the many mysteries of Christ's life, only a few are indicated by the Rosary in the form that has become generally established with the seal of the Church's approval. The selection was determined by the origin of the prayer, which was based on the number 150, the number of the Psalms in the Psalter.

I believe, however, that to bring out fully the Christological depth of the Rosary it would be suitable to make an addition to the traditional pattern which, while left to the freedom of individuals and communities, could broaden it to include *the mysteries of Christ's public ministry between his Baptism and his Passion.* In the course of those mysteries we contemplate important aspects of the person of Christ as the definitive revelation of God. Declared the beloved Son of the Father at the Baptism in the Jordan, Christ is the one who announces the coming of the Kingdom, bears witness to it in his works and proclaims its demands. It is during the years of his public ministry that *the mystery of Christ is most evidently a mystery of light:* "While I am in the world, I am the light of the world" (*Jn* 9:5).

Consequently, for the Rosary to become more fully a "compendium of the Gospel", it is fitting to add, following reflection on the Incarnation and the hidden life of Christ *(the joyful mysteries)* and before focusing on the sufferings of his Passion *(the sorrowful mysteries)* and the triumph of his Resurrection *(the glorious mysteries)*, a meditation on certain particularly significant moments in his public ministry *(the mysteries of light).* This addition of these new mysteries, without prejudice to any essential aspect of the prayer's traditional format, is meant to give it fresh life and to enkindle renewed interest in the Rosary's place within Christian spirituality as a true doorway to the depths of the Heart of Christ, ocean of joy and of light, of suffering and of glory.

The Joyful Mysteries

20. The first five decades, the "joyful mysteries", are marked by *the joy radiating from the event of the Incarnation.* This is clear from the very first mystery, the Annunciation, where Gabriel's greeting to the Virgin of Nazareth is linked to an invitation to messianic joy: "Rejoice, Mary". The whole of salvation history, in some sense the entire history of the world, has led up to this greeting. If it is the Father's plan to unite all things in Christ (cf. *Eph* 1:10), then the whole of the universe is in some way touched by the divine favour with which the Father looks upon Mary and makes her the Mother of his Son. The whole of humanity, in turn, is embraced by the fiat with which she readily agrees to the will of God.

Exultation is the keynote of the encounter with Elizabeth, where the sound of Mary's voice and the presence of Christ in her womb cause John to "leap for joy" (cf. *Lk* 1:44). Gladness also fills the scene in Bethlehem, when the birth of the divine Child, the Saviour of the world, is announced by the song of the angels and proclaimed to the shepherds as "news of great joy" (*Lk* 2:10).

The final two mysteries, while preserving this climate of joy, already point to the drama yet to come. The Presentation in the Temple not only expresses the joy of the Child's consecration and the ecstasy of the aged Simeon; it also records the prophecy that Christ will be a "sign of contradiction" for Israel and that a sword will pierce his mother's heart (cf *Lk* 2:34-35). Joy mixed with drama marks the fifth mystery, the finding of the twelve-year-old Jesus in the Temple. Here he appears in his divine wisdom as he listens and raises questions, already in effect one who "teaches". The revelation of his mystery as the Son wholly dedicated to his Father's affairs proclaims the radical nature of the Gospel, in which even the closest of human relationships are challenged by the absolute demands of the Kingdom. Mary and Joseph, fearful and anxious, "did not understand" his words (*Lk* 2:50).

To meditate upon the "joyful" mysteries, then, is to enter into the ultimate causes and the deepest meaning of Christian joy. It is to focus on the realism of the mystery of the Incarnation and on the obscure foreshadowing of the mystery of the saving Passion. Mary leads us to discover the secret of Christian joy, reminding us that Christianity is, first and foremost, *euangelion*, "good news", which has as its heart and its whole content the person of Jesus Christ, the Word made flesh, the one Saviour of the world.

The Mysteries of Light

21. Moving on from the infancy and the hidden life in Nazareth to the public life of Jesus, our contemplation brings us to those mysteries which may be called in a special way "mysteries of light". Certainly the whole mystery of Christ is a mystery of light. He is the "light of the world" (*Jn* 8:12). Yet this truth emerges in a special way during the years of his public life, when he proclaims the Gospel of the Kingdom. In proposing to the Christian community five significant

moments – "luminous" mysteries – during this phase of Christ's life, I think that the following can be fittingly singled out: (1) his Baptism in the Jordan, (2) his self-manifestation at the wedding of Cana, (3) his proclamation of the Kingdom of God, with his call to conversion, (4) his Transfiguration, and finally, (5) his institution of the Eucharist, as the sacramental expression of the Paschal Mystery.

Each of these mysteries is *a revelation of the Kingdom now present in the very person of Jesus.* The Baptism in the Jordan is first of all a mystery of light. Here, as Christ descends into the waters, the innocent one who became "sin" for our sake (cf. *2Cor* 5:21), the heavens open wide and the voice of the Father declares him the beloved Son (cf. *Mt* 3:17 and parallels), while the Spirit descends on him to invest him with the mission which he is to carry out. Another mystery of light is the first of the signs, given at Cana (cf. *Jn* 2:1- 12), when Christ changes water into wine and opens the hearts of the disciples to faith, thanks to the intervention of Mary, the first among believers. Another mystery of light is the preaching by which Jesus proclaims the coming of the Kingdom of God, calls to conversion (cf. *Mk* 1:15) and forgives the sins of all who draw near to him in humble trust (cf. *Mk* 2:3-13; *Lk* 7:47-48): the inauguration of that ministry of mercy which he continues to exercise until the end of the world, particularly through the Sacrament of Reconciliation which he has entrusted to his Church (cf. *Jn* 20:22-23). The mystery of light *par excellence* is the Transfiguration, traditionally believed to have taken place on Mount Tabor. The glory of the Godhead shines forth from the face of Christ as the Father commands the astonished Apostles to "listen to him" (cf. *Lk* 9:35 and parallels) and to prepare to experience with him the agony of the Passion, so as to come with him to the joy of the Resurrection and a life transfigured by the Holy Spirit. A final mystery of light is the institution of the Eucharist, in which Christ offers his body and blood as food under the signs of bread and wine, and testifies "to the end" his love for humanity (*Jn* 13:1), for whose salvation he will offer himself in sacrifice.

In these mysteries, apart from the miracle at Cana, *the presence of Mary remains in the background.* The Gospels make only the briefest reference to her occasional presence at one moment or other during the preaching of Jesus (cf. *Mk* 3:31-5; *Jn* 2:12), and they give no indication that she was present at the Last Supper and the institution of the

Eucharist. Yet the role she assumed at Cana in some way accompanies Christ throughout his ministry. The revelation made directly by the Father at the Baptism in the Jordan and echoed by John the Baptist is placed upon Mary's lips at Cana, and it becomes the great maternal counsel which Mary addresses to the Church of every age: "Do whatever he tells you" (*Jn* 2:5). This counsel is a fitting introduction to the words and signs of Christ's public ministry and it forms the Marian foundation of all the "mysteries of light".

The Sorrowful Mysteries

22. The Gospels give great prominence to the sorrowful mysteries of Christ. From the beginning Christian piety, especially during the Lenten devotion of the *Way of the Cross*, has focused on the individual moments of the Passion, realizing that here is found *the culmination of the revelation of God's love* and the source of our salvation. The Rosary selects certain moments from the Passion, inviting the faithful to contemplate them in their hearts and to relive them. The sequence of meditations begins with Gethsemane, where Christ experiences a moment of great anguish before the will of the Father, against which the weakness of the flesh would be tempted to rebel. There Jesus encounters all the temptations and confronts all the sins of humanity, in order to say to the Father: "Not my will but yours be done" (*Lk* 22:42 and parallels). This "Yes" of Christ reverses the "No" of our first parents in the Garden of Eden. And the cost of this faithfulness to the Father's will is made clear in the following mysteries; by his scourging, his crowning with thorns, his carrying the Cross and his death on the Cross, the Lord is cast into the most abject suffering: *Ecce homo!*

This abject suffering reveals not only the love of God but also the meaning of man himself.

Ecce homo: the meaning, origin and fulfilment of man is to be found in Christ, the God who humbles himself out of love "even unto death, death on a cross" (*Phil* 2:8). The sorrowful mysteries help the believer to relive the death of Jesus, to stand at the foot of the Cross beside Mary, to enter with her into the depths of God's love for man and to experience all its life-giving power.

23. "The contemplation of Christ's face cannot stop at the image of the Crucified One. He is the Risen One!"[(29)] The Rosary has always expressed this knowledge born of faith and invited the believer to pass beyond the darkness of the Passion in order to gaze upon Christ's glory in the Resurrection and Ascension. Contemplating the Risen One, Christians *rediscover the reasons for their own faith* (cf. *1Cor* 15:14) and relive the joy not only of those to whom Christ appeared – the Apostles, Mary Magdalene and the disciples on the road to Emmaus – but also *the joy of Mary,* who must have had an equally intense experience of the new life of her glorified Son. In the Ascension, Christ was raised in glory to the right hand of the Father, while Mary herself would be raised to that same glory in the Assumption, enjoying beforehand, by a unique privilege, the destiny reserved for all the just at the resurrection of the dead. Crowned in glory – as she appears in the last glorious mystery – Mary shines forth as Queen of the Angels and Saints, the anticipation and the supreme realization of the eschatological state of the Church.

At the centre of this unfolding sequence of the glory of the Son and the Mother, the Rosary sets before us the third glorious mystery, Pentecost, which reveals the face of the Church as a family gathered together with Mary, enlivened by the powerful outpouring of the Spirit and ready for the mission of evangelization. The contemplation of this scene, like that of the other glorious mysteries, ought to lead the faithful to an ever greater appreciation of their new life in Christ, lived in the heart of the Church, a life of which the scene of Pentecost itself is the great "icon". The glorious mysteries thus lead the faithful to *greater hope for the eschatological goal* towards which they journey as members of the pilgrim People of God in history. This can only impel them to bear courageous witness to that "good news" which gives meaning to their entire existence.

From "mysteries" to the "Mystery": Mary's way

24. The cycles of meditation proposed by the Holy Rosary are by no means exhaustive, but they do bring to mind what is essential and they awaken in the soul a thirst for a knowledge of Christ continually

nourished by the pure source of the Gospel. Every individual event in the life of Christ, as narrated by the Evangelists, is resplendent with the Mystery that surpasses all understanding (cf. *Eph* 3:19): the Mystery of the Word made flesh, in whom "all the fullness of God dwells bodily" (*Col* 2:9). For this reason the *Catechism of the Catholic Church* places great emphasis on the mysteries of Christ, pointing out that "everything in the life of Jesus is a sign of his Mystery".[30] The *"duc in altum"* of the Church of the third millennium will be determined by the ability of Christians to enter into the "perfect knowledge of God's mystery, of Christ, in whom are hidden all the treasures of wisdom and knowledge" (*Col* 2:2-3). The Letter to the Ephesians makes this heartfelt prayer for all the baptized: "May Christ dwell in your hearts through faith, so that you, being rooted and grounded in love, may have power... to know the love of Christ which surpasses knowledge, that you may be filled with all the fullness of God" (3:17-19).

The Rosary is at the service of this ideal; it offers the "secret" which leads easily to a profound and inward knowledge of Christ. We might call it *Mary's way*. It is the way of the example of the Virgin of Nazareth, a woman of faith, of silence, of attentive listening. It is also the way of a Marian devotion inspired by knowledge of the inseparable bond between Christ and his Blessed Mother: *the mysteries of Christ* are also in some sense *the mysteries of his Mother*, even when they do not involve her directly, for she lives from him and through him. By making our own the words of the Angel Gabriel and Saint Elizabeth contained in the *Hail Mary,* we find ourselves constantly drawn to seek out afresh in Mary, in her arms and in her heart, the "blessed fruit of her womb" (cf *Lk* 1:42).

Mystery of Christ, mystery of man

25. In my testimony of 1978 mentioned above, where I described the Rosary as my favourite prayer, I used an idea to which I would like to return. I said then that "the simple prayer of the Rosary marks the rhythm of human life".[31]

In the light of what has been said so far on the mysteries of Christ, it is not difficult to go deeper into this *anthropological significance* of the Rosary, which is far deeper than may appear at first sight. Anyone who contemplates Christ through the various stages of his life cannot fail to perceive in him *the truth about man*. This is the great affirmation of the Second Vatican Council which I have so often discussed in my own teaching since the Encyclical Letter *Redemptor Hominis:* "it is only in the mystery of the Word made flesh that the mystery of man is seen in its true light".[(32)] The Rosary helps to open up the way to this light. Following in the path of Christ, in whom man's path is "recapitulated",[(33)] revealed and redeemed, believers come face to face with the image of the true man. Contemplating Christ's birth, they learn of the sanctity of life; seeing the household of Nazareth, they learn the original truth of the family according to God's plan; listening to the Master in the mysteries of his public ministry, they find the light which leads them to enter the Kingdom of God; and following him on the way to Calvary, they learn the meaning of salvific suffering. Finally, contemplating Christ and his Blessed Mother in glory, they see the goal towards which each of us is called, if we allow ourselves to be healed and transformed by the Holy Spirit. It could be said that each mystery of the Rosary, carefully meditated, sheds light on the mystery of man.

At the same time, it becomes natural to bring to this encounter with the sacred humanity of the Redeemer all the problems, anxieties, labours and endeavours which go to make up our lives. "Cast your burden on the Lord and he will sustain you" (*Ps* 55:23). To pray the Rosary is to hand over our burdens to the merciful hearts of Christ and his Mother. Twenty-five years later, thinking back over the difficulties which have also been part of my exercise of the Petrine ministry, I feel the need to say once more, as a warm invitation to everyone to experience it personally: the Rosary does indeed "mark the rhythm of human life", bringing it into harmony with the "rhythm" of God's own life, in the joyful communion of the Holy Trinity, our life's destiny and deepest longing.

CHAPTER III
"For Me, to Live is Christ"

The Rosary, a way of assimilating the mystery

26. Meditation on the mysteries of Christ is proposed in the Rosary by means of a method designed to assist in their assimilation. It is a method *based on repetition*. This applies above all to the *Hail Mary*, repeated ten times in each mystery. If this repetition is considered superficially, there could be a temptation to see the Rosary as a dry and boring exercise. It is quite another thing, however, when the Rosary is thought of as an outpouring of that love which tirelessly returns to the person loved with expressions similar in their content but ever fresh in terms of the feeling pervading them.

In Christ, God has truly assumed a "heart of flesh". Not only does God have a divine heart, rich in mercy and in forgiveness, but also a human heart, capable of all the stirrings of affection. If we needed evidence for this from the Gospel, we could easily find it in the touching dialogue between Christ and Peter after the Resurrection: "Simon, son of John, do you love me?" Three times this question is put to Peter, and three times he gives the reply: "Lord, you know that I love you" (cf. *Jn* 21:15-17). Over and above the specific meaning of this passage, so important for Peter's mission, none can fail to recognize the beauty of this triple repetition, in which the insistent request and the corresponding reply are expressed in terms familiar from the universal experience of human love. To understand the Rosary, one has to enter into the psychological dynamic proper to love.

One thing is clear: although the repeated *Hail Mary* is addressed directly to Mary, it is to Jesus that the act of love is ultimately directed, with her and through her. The repetition is nourished by the desire to be conformed ever more completely to Christ, the true programme of the Christian life. Saint Paul expressed this project with words of fire: "For me to live is Christ and to die is gain" (*Phil* 1:21). And again: "It is no longer I that live, but Christ lives in me" (*Gal* 2:20). The Rosary helps us to be conformed ever more closely to Christ until we attain true holiness.

A valid method...

27. We should not be surprised that our relationship with Christ makes use of a method. God communicates himself to us respecting our human nature and its vital rhythms. Hence, while Christian spirituality is familiar with the most sublime forms of mystical silence in which images, words and gestures are all, so to speak, superseded by an intense and ineffable union with God, it normally engages the whole person in all his complex psychological, physical and relational reality.

This becomes apparent *in the Liturgy*. Sacraments and sacramentals are structured as a series of rites which bring into play all the dimensions of the person. The same applies to non-liturgical prayer. This is confirmed by the fact that, in the East, the most characteristic prayer of Christological meditation, centred on the words "Lord Jesus Christ, Son of God, have mercy on me, a sinner"[34] is traditionally linked to the rhythm of breathing; while this practice favours perseverance in the prayer, it also in some way embodies the desire for Christ to become the breath, the soul and the "all" of one's life.

... which can nevertheless be improved

28. I mentioned in my Apostolic Letter *Novo Millennio Ineunte* that the West is now experiencing *a renewed demand for meditation*, which at times leads to a keen interest in aspects of other religions.[35] Some Christians, limited in their knowledge of the Christian contemplative tradition, are attracted by those forms of prayer. While the latter contain many elements which are positive and at times compatible with Christian experience, they are often based on ultimately unacceptable premises. Much in vogue among these approaches are methods aimed at attaining a high level of spiritual concentration by using techniques of a psychophysical, repetitive and symbolic nature. The Rosary is situated within this broad gamut of religious phenomena, but it is distinguished by characteristics of its own which correspond to specifically Christian requirements.

In effect, the Rosary is simply a *method of contemplation*. As a method, it serves as a means to an end and cannot become an end in itself. All the same, as the fruit of centuries of experience, this method should not be undervalued. In its favour one could cite the experience of countless Saints. This is not to say, however, that the method cannot be improved. Such is the intent of the addition of the new series of *mysteria lucis* to the overall cycle of mysteries and of the few suggestions which I am proposing in this Letter regarding its manner of recitation. These suggestions, while respecting the well-established structure of this prayer, are intended to help the faithful to understand it in the richness of its symbolism and in harmony with the demands of daily life. Otherwise there is a risk that the Rosary would not only fail to produce the intended spiritual effects, but even that the beads, with which it is usually said, could come to be regarded as some kind of amulet or magic object, thereby radically distorting their meaning and function.

Announcing each mystery

29. Announcing each mystery, and perhaps even using a suitable icon to portray it, is as it were *to open up a scenario* on which to focus our attention. The words direct the imagination and the mind towards a particular episode or moment in the life of Christ. In the Church's traditional spirituality, the veneration of icons and the many devotions appealing to the senses, as well as the method of prayer proposed by Saint Ignatius of Loyola in the Spiritual Exercises, make use of visual and imaginative elements (the *compositio loci*), judged to be of great help in concentrating the mind on the particular mystery. This is a methodology, moreover, which *corresponds to the inner logic of the Incarnation*: in Jesus, God wanted to take on human features. It is through his bodily reality that we are led into contact with the mystery of his divinity.

This need for concreteness finds further expression in the announcement of the various mysteries of the Rosary. Obviously these mysteries neither replace the Gospel nor exhaust its content. The Rosary, therefore, is no substitute for *lectio divina*; on the contrary, it presupposes and promotes it. Yet, even though the mysteries contemplated in the Rosary, even with the addition of the *mysteria lucis*, do no more than outline the fundamental elements of the life of Christ, they easily draw the mind to a more expansive reflection on the rest of the Gospel, especially when the Rosary is prayed in a setting of prolonged recollection.

Listening to the word of God

30. In order to supply a Biblical foundation and greater depth to our meditation, it is helpful to follow the announcement of the mystery with *the proclamation of a related Biblical passage*, long or short, depending on the circumstances. No other words can ever match the efficacy of the inspired word. As we listen, we are certain that this is the word of God, spoken for today and spoken "for me".

If received in this way, the word of God can become part of the Rosary's methodology of repetition without giving rise to the ennui derived from the simple recollection of something already well known. It is not a matter of recalling information but of *allowing God to speak*. In certain solemn communal celebrations, this word can be appropriately illustrated by a brief commentary.

Silence

31. *Listening and meditation are nourished by silence.* After the announcement of the mystery and the proclamation of the word, it is fitting to pause and focus one's attention for a suitable period of time on the mystery concerned, before moving into vocal prayer. A discovery of the importance of silence is one of the secrets of practicing contemplation and meditation. One drawback of a society dominated by technology and the mass media is the fact that silence becomes increasingly difficult to achieve. Just as moments of silence are recommended in the Liturgy, so too in the recitation of the Rosary it is fitting to pause briefly after listening to the word of God, while the mind focuses on the content of a particular mystery.

The "Our Father"

32. After listening to the word and focusing on the mystery, it is natural *for the mind to be lifted up towards the Father*. In each of his mysteries, Jesus always leads us to the Father, for as he rests in the Father's bosom (cf. *Jn* 1:18) he is continually turned towards him. He wants us to share in his intimacy with the Father, so that we can say with him: "Abba, Father" (*Rom* 8:15; *Gal* 4:6). By virtue of his relationship to the Father he makes us brothers and sisters of himself and of one another,

communicating to us the Spirit which is both his and the Father's. Acting as a kind of foundation for the Christological and Marian meditation which unfolds in the repetition of the *Hail Mary*, the *Our Father* makes meditation upon the mystery, even when carried out in solitude, an ecclesial experience.

The ten "Hail Marys"

33. This is the most substantial element in the Rosary and also the one which makes it a Marian prayer *par excellence*. Yet when the *Hail Mary* is properly understood, we come to see clearly that its Marian character is not opposed to its Christological character, but that it actually emphasizes and increases it. The first part of the *Hail Mary*, drawn from the words spoken to Mary by the Angel Gabriel and by Saint Elizabeth, is a contemplation in adoration of the mystery accomplished in the Virgin of Nazareth. These words express, so to speak, the wonder of heaven and earth; they could be said to give us a glimpse of God's own wonderment as he contemplates his "masterpiece" – the Incarnation of the Son in the womb of the Virgin Mary. If we recall how, in the Book of Genesis, God "saw all that he had made" (*Gen* 1:31), we can find here an echo of that "pathos with which God, at the dawn of creation, looked upon the work of his hands".[36] The repetition of the *Hail Mary* in the Rosary gives us a share in God's own wonder and pleasure: in jubilant amazement we acknowledge the greatest miracle of history. Mary's prophecy here finds its fulfilment: "Henceforth all generations will call me blessed" (*Lk* 1:48).

The centre of gravity in the *Hail Mary*, the hinge as it were which joins its two parts, is *the name of Jesus*. Sometimes, in hurried recitation, this centre of gravity can be overlooked, and with it the connection to the mystery of Christ being contemplated. Yet it is precisely the emphasis given to the name of Jesus and to his mystery that is the sign of a meaningful and fruitful recitation of the Rosary. Pope Paul VI drew attention, in his Apostolic Exhortation *Marialis Cultus*, to the custom in certain regions of highlighting the name of Christ by the addition of a clause referring to the mystery being contemplated.[37] This is a praiseworthy custom, especially during public recitation. It gives forceful expression to our faith in Christ, directed to the different moments of the Redeemer's life. It is at once a *profession of faith* and an aid in concentrating our meditation, since it facilitates the process of assimilation to the mystery of Christ inherent in the repetition of the *Hail Mary*. When we repeat the name of Jesus – the only name given to us by which we may hope for salvation (cf. *Acts* 4:12) – in close association with the name of his Blessed Mother, almost as if it were done at her suggestion, we set out on a path of assimilation meant to help us enter more deeply into the life of Christ.

From Mary's uniquely privileged relationship with Christ, which makes her the Mother of God, *Theotókos*, derives the forcefulness of the appeal we make to her in the second half of the prayer, as we entrust to her maternal intercession our lives and the hour of our death.

The "Gloria"

34. Trinitarian doxology is the goal of all Christian contemplation. For Christ is the way that leads us to the Father in the Spirit. If we travel this way to the end, we repeatedly encounter the mystery of the three divine Persons, to whom all praise, worship and thanksgiving are due. It is important that the *Gloria, the high-point of contemplation*, be given due prominence in the Rosary. In public recitation it could be sung, as a way of giving proper emphasis to the essentially Trinitarian structure of all Christian prayer.

To the extent that meditation on the mystery is attentive and profound, and to the extent that it is enlivened – from one *Hail Mary* to another – by love for Christ and for Mary, the glorification of the Trinity at the end of each decade, far from being a perfunctory conclusion, takes on its proper contemplative tone, raising the mind as it were to the heights of heaven and enabling us in some way to relive the experience of Tabor, a foretaste of the contemplation yet to come: "It is good for us to be here!" (*Lk* 9:33).

The concluding short prayer

35. In current practice, the Trinitarian doxology is followed by a brief concluding prayer which varies according to local custom. Without in any way diminishing the value of such invocations, it is worthwhile to note that the contemplation of the mysteries could better express

their full spiritual fruitfulness if an effort were made to conclude each mystery with a prayer for the fruits specific to that particular mystery. In this way the Rosary would better express its connection with the Christian life. One fine liturgical prayer suggests as much, inviting us to pray that, by meditation on the mysteries of the Rosary, we may come to "imitate what they contain and obtain what they promise".[(38)]

Such a final prayer could take on a legitimate variety of forms, as indeed it already does. In this way the Rosary can be better adapted to different spiritual traditions and different Christian communities. It is to be hoped, then, that appropriate formulas will be widely circulated, after due pastoral discernment and possibly after experimental use in centres and shrines particularly devoted to the Rosary, so that the People of God may benefit from an abundance of authentic spiritual riches and find nourishment for their personal contemplation.

The Rosary beads

36. The traditional aid used for the recitation of the Rosary is the set of beads. At the most superficial level, the beads often become a simple counting mechanism to mark the succession of *Hail Marys*. Yet they can also take on a symbolism which can give added depth to contemplation.

Here the first thing to note is the way *the beads converge upon the Crucifix*, which both opens and closes the unfolding sequence of prayer. The life and prayer of believers is centred upon Christ. Everything begins from him, everything leads towards him, everything, through him, in the Holy Spirit, attains to the Father.

As a counting mechanism, marking the progress of the prayer, the beads evoke the unending path of contemplation and of Christian perfection. Blessed Bartolo Longo saw them also as a "chain" which links us to God. A chain, yes, but a sweet chain; for sweet indeed is the bond to God who is also our Father. A "filial" chain which puts us in tune with Mary, the "handmaid of the Lord" (*Lk* 1:38) and, most of all, with Christ himself, who, though he was in the form of God, made himself a "servant" out of love for us (*Phil* 2:7).

A fine way to expand the symbolism of the beads is to let them remind us of our many relationships, of the bond of communion and fraternity which unites us all in Christ.

The opening and closing

37. At present, in different parts of the Church, there are many ways to introduce the Rosary. In some places, it is customary to begin with the opening words of Psalm 70: "O God, come to my aid; O Lord, make haste to help me", as if to nourish in those who are praying a humble awareness of their own insufficiency. In other places, the Rosary begins with the recitation of the Creed, as if to make the profession of faith the basis of the contemplative journey about to be undertaken. These and similar customs, to the extent that they prepare the mind for contemplation, are all equally legitimate. The Rosary is then ended with a prayer for the intentions of the Pope, as if to expand the vision of the one praying to embrace all the needs of the Church. It is precisely in order to encourage this ecclesial dimension of the Rosary that the Church has seen fit to grant indulgences to those who recite it with the required dispositions.

If prayed in this way, the Rosary truly becomes a spiritual itinerary in which Mary acts as Mother, Teacher and Guide, sustaining the faithful by her powerful intercession. Is it any wonder, then, that the soul feels the need, after saying this prayer and experiencing so profoundly the motherhood of Mary, to burst forth in praise of the Blessed Virgin, either in that splendid prayer the *Salve Regina* or in the *Litany of Loreto*? This is the crowning moment of an inner journey which has brought the faithful into living contact with the mystery of Christ and his Blessed Mother.

Distribution over time

38. The Rosary can be recited in full every day, and there are those who most laudably do so. In this way it fills with prayer the days of many a contemplative, or keeps company with the sick and the elderly who have abundant time at their disposal. Yet it is clear – and this applies all the more if the new series of *mysteria lucis* is included – that many people will not be able to recite more than a part of the Rosary, according to a certain weekly pattern. This weekly distribution has the

effect of giving the different days of the week a certain spiritual "colour", by analogy with the way in which the Liturgy colours the different seasons of the liturgical year.

According to current practice, Monday and Thursday are dedicated to the "joyful mysteries", Tuesday and Friday to the "sorrowful mysteries", and Wednesday, Saturday and Sunday to the "glorious mysteries". Where might the "mysteries of light" be inserted? If we consider that the "glorious mysteries" are said on both Saturday and Sunday, and that Saturday has always had a special Marian flavour, the second weekly meditation on the "joyful mysteries", mysteries in which Mary's presence is especially pronounced, could be moved to Saturday. Thursday would then be free for meditating on the "mysteries of light".

This indication is not intended to limit a rightful freedom in personal and community prayer, where account needs to be taken of spiritual and pastoral needs and of the occurrence of particular liturgical celebrations which might call for suitable adaptations. What is really important is that the Rosary should always be seen and experienced as a path of contemplation. In the Rosary, in a way similar to what takes place in the Liturgy, the Christian week, centred on Sunday, the day of Resurrection, becomes a journey through the mysteries of the life of Christ, and he is revealed in the lives of his disciples as the Lord of time and of history.

CONCLUSION

"Blessed Rosary of Mary, sweet chain linking us to God"

39. What has been said so far makes abundantly clear the richness of this traditional prayer, which has the simplicity of a popular devotion but also the theological depth of a prayer suited to those who feel the need for deeper contemplation.

The Church has always attributed particular efficacy to this prayer, entrusting to the Rosary, to its choral recitation and to its constant practice, the most difficult problems. At times when Christianity itself seemed under threat, its deliverance was attributed to the power of this prayer, and Our Lady of the Rosary was acclaimed as the one whose intercession brought salvation.

Today I willingly entrust to the power of this prayer – as I mentioned at the beginning – the cause of peace in the world and the cause of the family.

Peace

40. The grave challenges confronting the world at the start of this new Millennium lead us to think that only an intervention from on high, capable of guiding the hearts of those living in situations of conflict and those governing the destinies of nations, can give reason to hope for a brighter future.

The Rosary is by its nature a prayer for peace, since it consists in the contemplation of Christ, the Prince of Peace, the one who is "our peace" (*Eph* 2:14). Anyone who assimilates the mystery of Christ – and this is clearly the goal of the Rosary – learns the secret of peace and makes it his life's project. Moreover, by virtue of its meditative character, with the tranquil succession of *Hail Marys*, the Rosary has a peaceful effect on those who pray it, disposing them to receive and experience in their innermost depths, and to spread around them, that true peace which is the special gift of the Risen Lord (cf. *Jn* 14:27; 20.21).

The Rosary is also a prayer for peace because of the fruits of charity which it produces. When prayed well in a truly meditative way, the Rosary leads to an encounter with Christ in his mysteries and so cannot fail to draw attention to the face of Christ in others, especially in the most afflicted. How could one possibly contemplate the mystery of the Child of Bethlehem, in the joyful mysteries, without experiencing the desire to welcome, defend and promote life, and to shoulder the burdens of suffering children all over the world? How could one possibly follow in the footsteps of Christ the Revealer, in the mysteries of light, without resolving to bear witness to his "Beatitudes" in daily life? And how could one contemplate Christ carrying the Cross and Christ Crucified, without feeling the need to act as a "Simon of Cyrene" for our brothers and sisters weighed down by grief or crushed by despair? Finally, how could one possibly gaze upon the glory of the Risen Christ or of Mary Queen of Heaven, without yearning to make this world more beautiful, more just, more closely conformed to God's plan?

In a word, by focusing our eyes on Christ, the Rosary also makes us peacemakers in the world. By its nature as an insistent choral petition in harmony with Christ's invitation to "pray ceaselessly" (*Lk* 18:1), the Rosary allows us to hope that, even today, the difficult "battle" for peace can be won. Far from offering an escape from the problems of the world, the Rosary obliges us to see them with responsible and generous eyes, and obtains for us the strength to face them with the certainty of God's help and the firm intention of bearing witness in every situation to "love, which binds everything together in perfect harmony" (*Col* 3:14).

The family: parents...

41. As a prayer for peace, the Rosary is also, and always has been, *a prayer of and for the family.* At one time this prayer was particularly dear to Christian families, and it certainly brought them closer together. It is important not to lose this precious inheritance. We need to return to the practice of family prayer and prayer for families, continuing to use the Rosary.

In my Apostolic Letter *Novo Millennio Ineunte* I encouraged the celebration of the *Liturgy of the Hours* by the lay faithful in the ordinary life of parish communities and Christian groups;[(39)] I now wish to do the same for the Rosary. These two paths of Christian contemplation are not mutually exclusive; they complement one another. I would therefore ask those who devote themselves to the pastoral care of families to recommend heartily the recitation of the Rosary.

The family that prays together stays together. The Holy Rosary, by age-old tradition, has shown itself particularly effective as a prayer which brings the family together. Individual family members, in turning their eyes towards Jesus, also regain the ability to look one another in the eye, to communicate, to show solidarity, to forgive one another and to see their covenant of love renewed in the Spirit of God.

Many of the problems facing contemporary families, especially in economically developed societies, result from their increasing difficulty in communicating. Families seldom manage to come together, and the rare occasions when they do are often taken up with watching television. To return to the recitation of the family Rosary means filling daily life with very different images, images of the mystery of salvation: the image of the Redeemer, the image of his most Blessed Mother. The family that recites the Rosary together reproduces something of the atmosphere of the household of Nazareth: its members place Jesus at the centre, they share his joys and sorrows, they place their needs and their plans in his hands, they draw from him the hope and the strength to go on.

<h3 style="text-align:center">... and children</h3>

42. It is also beautiful and fruitful to entrust to this prayer *the growth and development of children*. Does the Rosary not follow the life of Christ, from his conception to his death, and then to his Resurrection and his glory? Parents are finding it ever more difficult to follow the lives of their children as they grow to maturity. In a society of advanced technology, of mass communications and globalization, everything has become hurried, and the cultural distance between generations is growing ever greater. The most diverse messages and the most unpredictable experiences rapidly make their way into the lives of children and adolescents, and parents can become quite anxious about the dangers their children face. At times parents suffer acute disappointment at the failure of their children to resist the seductions of the drug culture, the lure of an unbridled hedonism, the temptation to violence, and the manifold expressions of meaninglessness and despair.

To pray the Rosary *for children*, and even more, *with children*, training them from their earliest years to experience this daily "pause for prayer" with the family, is admittedly not the solution to every problem, but it is a spiritual aid which should not be underestimated. It could be objected that the Rosary seems hardly suited to the taste of children and young people of today. But perhaps the objection is directed to an impoverished method of praying it. Furthermore, without prejudice to the Rosary's basic structure, there is nothing to stop children and young people from praying it – either within the family or in groups – with appropriate symbolic and practical aids to understanding and appreciation. Why not try it? With God's help, a pastoral approach to youth which is positive, impassioned and creative – as shown by the World Youth Days! – is capable of achieving quite remarkable results. If the Rosary is well presented, I am sure that young people will once more surprise adults by the way they make this prayer their own and recite it with the enthusiasm typical of their age group.

The Rosary, a treasure to be rediscovered

43. Dear brothers and sisters! A prayer so easy and yet so rich truly deserves to be rediscovered by the Christian community. Let us do so, especially this year, as a means of confirming the direction outlined in my Apostolic Letter *Novo Millennio Ineunte*, from which the pastoral plans of so many particular Churches have drawn inspiration as they look to the immediate future.

I turn particularly to you, my dear Brother Bishops, priests and deacons, and to you, pastoral agents in your different ministries: through your own personal experience of the beauty of the Rosary, may you come to promote it with conviction.

I also place my trust in you, theologians: by your sage and rigorous reflection, rooted in the word of God and sensitive to the lived experience of the Christian people, may you help them to discover the Biblical foundations, the spiritual riches and the pastoral value of this traditional prayer.

I count on you, consecrated men and women, called in a particular way to contemplate the face of Christ at the school of Mary.

I look to all of you, brothers and sisters of every state of life, to you, Christian families, to you, the sick and elderly, and to you, young people: *confidently take up the Rosary once again*. Rediscover the Rosary in the light of Scripture, in harmony with the Liturgy, and in the context of your daily lives.

May this appeal of mine not go unheard! At the start of the twenty-fifth year of my Pontificate, I entrust this Apostolic Letter to the loving hands of the Virgin Mary, *prostrating myself in spirit before her image in the splendid Shrine built for her by Blessed Bartolo Longo*, the apostle of the Rosary. I willingly make my own the touching words with which he concluded his well-known *Supplication to the Queen of the Holy Rosary*: "O Blessed Rosary of Mary, sweet chain which unites us to God, bond of love which unites us to the angels, tower of salvation against the assaults of Hell, safe port in our universal shipwreck, we will never abandon you. You will be our comfort in the hour of death: yours our final kiss as life ebbs away. And the last word from our lips will be your sweet name, O Queen of the Rosary of Pompei, O dearest Mother, O Refuge of Sinners, O Sovereign Consoler of the Afflicted. May you be everywhere blessed, today and always, on earth and in heaven".

Source: From the Vatican, on the 16th day of October in the year 2002, the beginning of the twenty-fifth year of my Pontificate. **JOHN PAUL II.**

SOURCE CITATIONS

(1) Pastoral Constitution on the Church in the Modern World Gaudium et Spes, 45.
(2) Pope Paul VI, Apostolic Exhortation Marialis Cultus (2 February 1974), 42: AAS 66 (1974), 153.
(3) Cf. Acta Leonis XIII, 3 (1884), 280-289.
(4) Particularly worthy of note is his Apostolic Epistle on the Rosary Il religioso convegno (29 September 1961): AAS 53 (1961), 641-647.
(5) Angelus: Insegnamenti di Giovanni Paolo II, I (1978): 75-76.
(6) AAS 93 (2001), 285.
(7) During the years of preparation for the Council, Pope John XXIII did not fail to encourage the Christian community to recite the Rosary for the success of this ecclesial event: cf. Letter to the Cardinal Vicar (28 September 1960): AAS 52 (1960), 814-816.
(8) Dogmatic Constitution on the Church Lumen Gentium, 66.
(9) No. 32: AAS 93 (2001), 288.
(10) Ibid., 33: loc. cit., 289.
(11) It is well-known and bears repeating that private revelations are not the same as public revelation, which is binding on the whole Church. It is the task of the Magisterium to discern and recognize the authenticity and value of private revelations for the piety of the faithful.
(12) The Secret of the Rosary.
(13) Blessed Bartolo Longo, Storia del Santuario di Pompei, Pompei, 1990, 59.
(14) Apostolic Exhortation Marialis Cultus (2 February 1974), 47: AAS (1974), 156.
(15) Constitution on the Sacred Liturgy Sacrosanctum Concilium, 10.
(16) Ibid., 12.
(17) Second Vatican Ecumenical Council, Dogmatic Constitution on the Church Lumen Gentium, 58.

(18) I Quindici Sabati del Santissimo Rosario, 27th ed., Pompei, 1916, 27.

(19) Second Vatican Ecumenical Council, Dogmatic Constitution on the Church Lumen Gentium, 53.

(20) Ibid., 60.

(21) Cf. First Radio Address Urbi et Orbi (17 October 1978): AAS 70 (1978), 927.

(22) Treatise on True Devotion to the Blessed Virgin Mary.

(23) Catechism of the Catholic Church, 2679.

(24) Ibid., 2675.

(25) The Supplication to the Queen of the Holy Rosary was composed by Blessed Bartolo Longo in 1883 in response to the appeal of Pope Leo XIII, made in his first Encyclical on the Rosary, for the spiritual commitment of all Catholics in combating social ills. It is solemnly recited twice yearly, in May and October.

(26) Divina Commedia, Paradiso XXXIII, 13-15.

(27) John Paul II, Apostolic Letter Novo Millennio Ineunte (6 January 2001), 20: AAS 93 (2001), 279.

(28) Apostolic Exhortation Marialis Cultus (2 February 1974), 46: AAS 6 (1974), 155.

(29) John Paul II, Apostolic Letter Novo Millennio Ineunte (6 January 2001), 28: AAS 93 (2001), 284.

(30) No. 515.

(31) Angelus Message of 29 October 1978 : Insegnamenti, I (1978), 76.

(32) Second Vatican Ecumenical Council, Pastoral Constitution on the Church in the Modern World Gaudium et Spes, 22.

(33) Cf. Saint Irenaeus of Lyons, Adversus Haereses, III, 18, 1: PG 7, 932.

(34) Catechism of the Catholic Church, 2616.

(35) Cf. No. 33: AAS 93 (2001), 289.

(36) John Paul II, Letter to Artists (4 April 1999), 1: AAS 91 (1999), 1155.

(37) Cf. No. 46: AAS 66 (1974), 155. This custom has also been recently praised by the Congregation for Divine Worship and for the Discipline of the Sacraments in its Direttorio su pietà popolare e liturgia. Principi e orientamenti (17 December 2001), 201, Vatican City, 2002, 165.

(38) "...concede, quaesumus, ut haec mysteria sacratissimo beatae Mariae Virginis Rosario recolentes, et imitemur quod continent, et quod promittunt assequamur". Missale Romanum 1960, in festo B.M. Virginis a Rosario.

(39) Cf. No. 34: AAS 93 (2001), 290.